Faithful God

Faithful Good

by

John R. Clarke

This book is dedicated to our Heavenly Father, the Almighty and everlasting God, to our Lord and Saviour Jesus Christ, and to the blessed anointing of the Holy Spirit, who is our comforter and teacher. May you, the reader, receive grace and peace and find many blessings among the pages of this book.

I also dedicate this book to my wonderful wife, Kalpna, and our son, Sam. Both are a great gift and a blessing from God. The book is also dedicated to our friends at Norreys Church, Wokingham, and especially Ralph Higson whose continued support and encouragement have been a special blessing to both myself and my family.

Contents

Preface

ALL OF US WANT to be free and to come to know what it means to be truly free. Jesus offered us the opportunity to know the truth, and that his truth would set us free, but what does it mean to be truly free? It means being set free to be the person God created us to be, to be free from fear, from circumstances, from the strongholds that tell us that we can never achieve all that we want to achieve.

What is God really like? That is a question that everyone who is searching for a closer walk with God is looking to answer. Other questions and dilemmas that face us in the 21st century include what is God doing in the world and how should we react and respond in a world that seems out of control and on a slippery slope to despair? Closer examination of the word of God leads us to understand what is happening in our world and how God both views us, and the fact that he is in control of the world. God hasn't given up on mankind but is faithful to his promises and will bring us into a closer walk with him.

The book is aimed at Christians at all stages of their relationship with Christ. The book should also be of interest to those who are seeking to understand the basis of the truth that sets us free from the powers of darkness. Also, the book highlights the things that prevent us from fulfilling our God-given destiny.

The book provides an overview of who God is and why we can rely upon him regardless of the circumstances we find ourselves facing. A clearer understanding of the living God and his awesome power to deliver and rescue us from a world that is out of control, and becoming darker as we move towards the end of this age, will help us all to stand firm and know that God has plans for each of us. Those plans will give hope and a future and show that God's ultimate purpose is to bring us into a closer, more profound and deeper relationship with him.

The book provides exciting assurances of God's plan for each one of his children as we move toward the end of this age. God has also provided an insight into heaven and what it means to one day be in paradise with him.

—John R. Clarke

1.

Faithful God

IF SOMEONE TOLD YOU that God was coming to your house this evening for supper, what would you think? We would want to know what God was like and would he be the kind of God we would want to meet or should we run and hide? In finding out what God is like and who he is, we should start at the beginning.

In the beginning

In the beginning, there was God the Father, Jesus the Son and the Holy Spirit (Gen 1:1, Gen 1:26, Gen 3:22, John 1:1-3). The question arises—in the beginning of what? Definitely before the beginning of the world and before the beginning of the universes and cosmos. Even before the beginning of time, there was God. Indeed, time never existed before mankind inhabited the world.[1] Before man, the ingresses and egresses of the cosmos had

---

1. Neil Oliver. *A History of Ancient Britain*. Chapter 1: "Ice," pp. 1-3. Weidenfeld & Nicolson, London, UK, 2012.

no one to assess their age or to measure time. Others, like Stephen Hawking, note the possibility that time did not exist before the existence of the universe.[2] Indeed, scientists are struggling to come up with a unified theory of how the universe came into being and how it functions.[3] Furthermore, scientists have deduced that there is no such thing as absolute time, therefore, the universe has a beginning and an end.[4] Yet, there is a deep human longing for significance and a meaning to the purpose of why we are here.[5] The Bible confirmed over 2,000 years ago that there would be a new heaven and a new earth because the old earth no longer existed due to man's impact on the current earth (Revelation 21:1-2).

It would be interesting to speculate what God the Father, Jesus the Son and the Holy Spirit were doing before they created the cosmos, the universe and the earth, but we simply do not know. It is a mystery and something that we mere mortals cannot get our brains around. It is difficult for us to accept that God has always existed and that he has no beginning or end. The Holy Trinity, as Father, Son and Holy Spirit, has always been there which is comforting to know in the midst of the turmoil of the earth. The really good news is that the Triune God

---

2. Stephen Hawking. *A Brief History of Time: From the big bang to black holes*. Chapter 1: "Our picture of the universe," pp. 9-10. Bantam Books, London, reissued 2016.

3. Ibid., pp. 1-16.

4. Ibid., Chapter 2: "Space and time," pp. 17-39.

5. Alister McGrath. *Glimpsing the Face of God: The search for meaning in the universe*. Chapter 2: "Trying to make sense of things," pp. 14-24. Lion Publishing PLC, Oxford, England, 2002.

never changes; He is the same yesterday, today and forever (Revelation 4:8, Hebrew 13:8). In an uncertain world where things can change in an instant, it is good to know that the foundation of our belief is in a God who never changes. In the midst of the book of Lamentations, which describes the most horrific scenes following the fall of Jerusalem to the Babylonians and the most depraved actions of humans, we find hope (Lamentations 3: 21-23). God provides His faithful steadfast love which never ceases and His mercy never ends; indeed, they are renewed every day which shows God's continual love for His people. Regardless of the trials and tribulations that we face daily, and beyond the difficulties we face today, there is God.

Sinfulness and evil are a universal predicament of man and, without God, life is destined for a life of misery (Genesis 6:5, Ephesians 2:3).[6] Despite an unpredictable world full of atrocities, wars and rumours of wars, including ethnic cleansing, there is God, the same yesterday, today and forever. Jesus was sent into the world not to bring judgement and condemnation but to save the world from the evil that is so prominent within (John 3:17). God loved the world so much that He gave His most precious Son that whoever believed in Jesus would not perish but have eternal life (John 3:16). God's genuine love for the world, regardless of the evil therein, provides the basis for hope for all mankind. The foundation of our faith in

---

6. Lewis Bayly. *The Practice of Piety: Puritan devotional manual, directing a Christian how to live that he may please God.* Chapter 1: "Meditations on the miserable state of those not reconciled to God," pp. 2-22. Published by Amazon, 2015; originally published 1601.

God is that He loves us, that He hasn't abandoned us but rather He has plans for us that will not bring us harm but will provide us with hope and a future that is better than our present circumstances (Jeremiah 29:11). Assuredly, God has promised to rescue us from every evil attack and bring us home safe and sound to His heavenly kingdom (2 Timothy 4:18). He has promised to be a shield for us against all the harm the world can inflict (Psalm 18:30).

Unfaithfulness is a word that is becoming very common in our world as marriages break down, relationships fail or couples fall out under the pressures of life. During the Covid-19 pandemic in the UK, 22% of adults reported a relationship breakdown with family, friends, partners or colleagues.[7] The largest group experiencing relationships breaking down were those aged between 19 and 25 years, of whom 35% had experienced a breakdown in their relationships. Therefore, more than previous generations, we need to have someone in our lives who we can depend upon and rely upon and who is going to be faithful and to be there for us in the difficult situations we face in a world that appears out of control.

The attributes of God

Therefore, we need to ask who is the true Living God? Firstly, God is infinite. He has no beginning and no end, from everlasting to everlasting He is God (Psalm 90:2).

---

7. https://www.standard.co.uk/news/uk/relationship-breakdown-pandemic-uk-study-coronavirus-b950500.html

Geologists have found rocks that are over 500 million years old; mountain ranges such as the Pyrenees are dated as forming 65 million years ago and the Rocky Mountains were formed between 55 and 80 million years ago.[8, 9] Yet, before the mountains were created, God brought forth the earth (Psalm 90:2). Scientists claim that by their calculations, the earth is estimated to be between 4.4 and 4.5 billion years old yet God created it.[10] There is, equally, a good deal of evidence to suggest that the earth is much younger in terms of chronological years. However, it is worth reiterating that time is an invention of mankind and didn't exist before man invented it. The infinity of God cannot be measured in age or time because God is beyond the measurable and God lives outside of the limitations of time.[11] It is not possible for us as humans to grasp the infinitude of God; we simply cannot get our minds around the vastness that is God.[12]

We also struggle to imagine the immensity of God and God challenges us to provide answers to where we were when He laid the foundations of the earth and when He created the stars (Job 38:4-7). When looking at the

---

8. "The Geology of the Pyrenees." Accessed 25 February 2022. https://www.hikepyrenees.co.uk/geology-of-the-pyrenees/

9. "Rocky Mountains." *Wikipedia.* Accessed 25 February 2022. https://en.wikipedia.org/wiki/Rocky_Mountains

10. "The Age of the Earth." *National Geographic.* Accessed 25 February 2022. https://www.nationalgeographic.org/topics/resource-library-age-earth/

11. A. W. Tozer. *The Attributes of God: Volume 1; A Journey into the Father's Heart.* Chapter 1: "God's Infinitude," pp. 1-17. Christian Publications, Inc., Camp Hill, PA 1997.

12. A. W. Tozer. *The Knowledge of the Holy.* Chapter 8: "God's Infinitude," pp. 49-54. STL Productions Bromley, Kent, UK, 1977.

nature of the earth, we cannot comprehend how they came into being (Isaiah 40:12). The immensity of God can be seen in the vastness of the expanding universe and some solar systems are so immense that our solar system could simply vanish within their vastness.[13]

We cannot hide from God, He is everywhere (Psalm 139:7-10). He is forever present. God is self-existent and has no origin.[14] This is one of the attributes of God that we find most difficult to grasp because our finite minds think that everyone has to have a beginning, an origin and an end. The thought of God not having a beginning is more than we can grasp or imagine. God is simply I AM WHO I AM (Exodus 3:11-15). God's greatness is un-searchable (Psalm 145:3), God's thoughts are higher than our thoughts and beyond what we are capable of grasping (Isaiah 55:8-9). God is immortal (1 Timothy 6:16).[15] I would recommend the two volumes by A. W. Tozer on the attributes of God to get a full overview of the im-menseness of our God.[16] Some of the attributes of God that we haven't mentioned here include God's imma-nence, that God penetrates everything, God's perfection and holiness, omnipotence, transcendence, omniscience and immutability. In all, God's immense being is greater

---

13. A. W. Tozer. *The Attributes of God: Volume 1; A Journey into the Father's Heart.* Chapter 2: "God's Immensity," pp. 17-38.

14. A. W. Tozer. *The Attributes of God: Volume 2; Deeper into the Father's Heart.* Chapter 1: "God's self-existence," pp. 15-32. Christian Publica-tions, Inc., Camp Hill, PA 1997.

15. A. W. Tozer. *The Attributes of God: Volume 2; Deeper into the Father's Heart,* ibid. See the general chapter headings of this volume.

16. A. W. Tozer. *The Attributes of God: Volume 1, Volume 2.*

than we can grasp or imagine which leads us naturally to consider God's faithfulness towards us.

God's faithfulness

For those who know Jesus as their Lord and Saviour and have entrusted our lives to His care, there is much that we can expect from God. For those who believe in Jesus as their Lord and Saviour, God is faithful in welcoming us into His family (1 Corinth 1:9). God is also faithful in forgiving us from our sins and failures to live up to His perfect standards (1 John 1:9). We can have confidence that God is faithful that the blood of Jesus will cleanse our hearts and minds from our evil consciences (Hebrews 10:21-23). If we are faithful with the gifts that God has given us and use our talents to please God, then we can be confident that God will be able to call us His faithful servants for we will have run the race that leads to eternal life (Matthew 25:21). If we entrust our lives to God when we are suffering and going through bad experiences in life, then God, our creator, will be faithful in bringing us home to eternal life (1 Peter 4:19). God rewards our faithfulness to Him by being faithful with us (1 Thessalonians 5:23-24). Our God is faithful in keeping His promises to not only us but to our children and grandchildren even down to 1000 generations (Deuteronomy 7:9).

We worship God because He is faithful and we can rely on Him in the midst of mankind's troubles (Isaiah 25:1). As I write this, Russia has invaded Ukraine and as things are not going according to plan, Putin is threatening to use nuclear weapons. Jesus warned us that there would be wars and rumours of wars as the birth pangs of the end of the world (Matthew 24:6-8). However, we are not to be alarmed or worried by such threats because we can rely upon the protection of God from such threats and catastrophes. Whoever hears Jesus's words and believes in Him and God has the promise of eternal life (John 5:24). That is the promise of a faithful God; no matter what life brings our way, we can rely upon God. We can live a life in Christ by faith that He whom we have trusted will deliver the eternal life He has promised (Galatians 2:19-20). Jesus will give us eternal life that will never end or perish (John 10:28-30).

We should know that God is not like men and He never lies; we can rely upon Him because He is faithful (Numbers 23:19). God overflows with faithfulness and His glory cannot be surpassed by anything that man has ever witnessed or seen (Exodus 34:6). The faithfulness of God is a shield that protects us from all that life throws at us (Psalm 91:4). God has promised to protect us from disease, plagues, terror, from the destruction caused through war and from evil (Psalm 91:2-10). God's faithfulness endures throughout history and He can be relied upon in these dark days of the earth (Psalm 119:90). As parents, we worry and are concerned about the future of our children and grandchildren but God has promised to protect them to the 1000th generation in light of the deteriorating world and the geological changes in the earth brought about by global warming and mankind's greed. We can rely upon God to be true to His promises. Nothing can be compared to God's faithfulness which will continue forever (Psalm 89:5).

God is the foundation of life

Every house needs a good foundation otherwise it will fall down and collapse when storms come. (Matthew 7:24). Please note that it is not sufficient to just believe but we must act upon the words of God and put into action what the Lord Jesus is teaching us. We not only have to have Jesus's commands but we need to keep them (John 14:21-23). The word of God is the foundation we need to build our life upon. God wants to be our God and live among us and He wants us to be His people (Leviticus 26:11-12, Jeremiah 30:22; Jeremiah 31:33-34). The godly man has been redeemed through the grace of God and has become a new creation and the life we now live we live in Christ (Galatians 2:19). Jesus has freed us from our bondage by Satan.[17] God is not slow in His actions toward us and the Lord will come at the right time in history, without warning, in a blink of a human eye (2 Peter 3:9). Let us be awake and ready for His coming.

---

17. Lewis Bayly. *The Practice of Piety: Puritan devotional manual, directing a Christian how to live that he may please God.* Chapter 2: "Meditations on the blessed state of those reconciled to God," pp. 23-29. Published by Amazon 2015, originally published 1601.

Prayer

Dear Heavenly Father, you have called us into your family to be your children and to follow your ways. We are grateful that despite our shortcomings, you faithfully love us and have promised eternal life to all who call upon the name of Jesus. We rejoice and are glad that despite the uncertainties of the world, we can rely upon your faithfulness. You are our strong foundation; an ever-present help in times of trouble. Thank you for always being there for us and delivering us from the evil one. In Jesus's name we pray.

2.

Salvation comes from the Lord

PERHAPS THE MOST famous verse in the whole Bible is John 3:16 showing that God loved the world so much that He gave His most precious son Jesus to die for our sins, failings and iniquities and that all who believe in Jesus will be saved and have eternal life. However, the promise of salvation and eternal life comes with a stark warning that whoever prefers darkness and evil will be condemned and face an eternity in hell (John 3:19). The Bible provides two choices—to come into the light which is salvation through Jesus or to remain in the evil darkness and, quite literally, go to hell. The saddest part of the two options is that the Bible says that most of mankind opts to remain in their evil ways and reject God's love and offer of salvation. God promises that everyone who calls on the name of the Lord Jesus will be saved (Romans 10:13). Jesus is the door through which we can enter into God's Kingdom and be saved (John 10:9).

Jesus has clearly shown that He is the only way to the Father and nobody can be accepted by the Father apart from Jesus (John 14:6), a fact that is confirmed by the Apostles teaching (Acts 2:21, Acts 4:11-12, Acts 16:31).

How do we reconcile the fact of all who call upon the Lord will be saved with Jesus's declaration in Matthew 7:23 against those who claim to have cast out demons, performed miracles and prophesied in Jesus's name but Jesus stated that he never knew them? It is clear that these evil-doers did not call upon the name of the Lord and did not depend on the Lord for their actions. Rather, they acted out of their own interests and for their own glory and not for the glory of God.

Working out our salvation

We are instructed to work out our salvation as God works within us (Philippians 2:12-13). In reality, we are to allow God to change us. We know that those who are true followers of Jesus keep His commandments (John 14:15). A large part of keeping Jesus's commandments is that we love one another (John 13:34) which is a major sign that we are followers of Jesus (John 13:35). Loving one another will become more challenging as each generation passes; we are warned that as lawlessness increases, the love of many will grow cold (Matthew 24:12). As we watch the news that is beamed into our living rooms each evening through our televisions, we can see lawlessness manifested in anarchy, strife, turbulent times, turmoil, unrest, upheaval, uprising and an increase in criminality.

Our newspapers report that anarchy explodes across Europe as violent anti-lockdown to Covid-19 marches erupt across the continent.[18] Protests in America are reported to be a disguise for anarchy as those who are discriminated against because of the colour of their skin demonstrate through groups such as Black Lives Matter.[19] It is important to point out that racism is rife and is both wrong and brings a great deal of hurt and suffering to those who have been on the receiving end of it. Organizations such as Kick It Out are to be supported and respected as they fight to educate racists and bring an end to racism. If we genuinely love one another as Christ loved us, then there will be no racism as all men and women are equal in the eyes of God (Galatians 3:28). Climate change protestors, such as Insulate Britain, have also caused havoc and turmoil by blocking motorways in the UK and stopping thousands getting to work.[20] Parental control of teenagers and strife and rebellion in families are on the increase and make it difficult to have a loving homelife.[21]

---

18. Laura O'Callaghan. "Europe protests: Anarchy explodes across continent as violent anti-lockdown marches erupt." *Express.co.uk*, Oct 29, 2020. Accessed March 1, 2022. https://www.express.co.uk/news/world/1353782/europe-protests-coronavirus-lockdown-violence-latest-italy-france-germany

19. "Anarchy Disguised as Protest." *speakingaboutnews.com*. Accessed March 1, 2022. https://speakingaboutnews.com/anarchy-disguised-as-protest/

20. "M25 junctions blocked by Insulate Britain campaigners." *BBC News*. Accessed March 1, 2022. https://www.bbc.co.uk/news/uk-england-beds-bucks-herts-58543603

21. "Teenage rebellion starts at 10." *The Guardian*. Accessed March 1, 2022. https://www.theguardian.com/uk/2006/dec/24/deniscampbell.theobserver

The 58th Munich Security Conference called for unity in a time of upheaval caused by the prospect of war in Ukraine which started after the conference and is ongoing as I write, and conflict zones in other parts of the world.[22] The conference identified "a rising tide of mutually reinforcing crises" which not only included warzones but also the erosion of democracy, the climate crisis, the coronavirus pandemic and the dependency on critical technologies.

Christian identity

As Christians, we are called to love one another, even those we find difficult to love. Jesus's parable of the good Samaritan reinforced that what love means, in reality, is action and is practical (Luke 10:25-37) and the parable of the prodigal son underlines our Heavenly Father's love for us (Luke 15:11-32). By walking in love, we will become imitators of God (Ephesians 5:1) and as our love grows, we will finally become like Jesus when He returns in all His glory for the Saints (2 Thessalonians 1:10, 1 Thessalonians 4:16-17).

We are called to desire heavenly things and not chase after earthly rewards and recognition (Colossians 3:1). What should distinguish us from the world is not only our love for one another but that we seek for the guid-

---

22. *Unity in a Time of Upheaval: A Readout from the Munich Security Conference 2022.* Accessed March 1, 2022. https://securityconference.org/assets/01_Bilder_Inhalte/03_Medien/02_Publikationen/2022/MSB_Readout_UnityinaTimeofUpheaval_MSC22.pdf

ance of the Holy Spirit (Galatians 5:16-18). The fruit of the Holy Spirit should be evident in our lives (Galatians 5:22-23) and we should be joyful people regardless of our circumstances. To be joyful when we are suffering requires us to rise above our circumstances and rejoice that God has considered us worthy to share in His sufferings (1 Peter 4:13). The peace of God which passes all understanding should fill our hearts and minds and whatever lies before us, we should be at peace with God (Philippians 4:7). We should also grow in patience, however, in the 21st century, patience is lacking as we seek instant answers. However, the testing of our faith produces patience and perseverance (James 1:3-4). When people look at us, they should be able to see goodness, kindness, faithfulness, gentleness and self-control as these are the attributes that should set us apart from the world.

Salvation through trials

Because we belong to Jesus, the world will hate us as followers of Christ (John 15:18-19) and we were warned by Jesus that the world hates us because we are different. So, it should come as no surprise that the world hates us but Jesus has also promised that we will be able to overcome the world and its persecution (John 16:33). Paul Billheimer, in his book *Overcomers Through the Cross*, states that the throne of the universe is a cross.[23] Jesus

---

23. Paul E. Billheimer. *Overcomers Through the Cross.* Chapter 1: "The throne of the universe is a cross." Kingsway Publications, Eastbourne, UK, 1983.

challenged us to take up our cross and follow Him (Matthew 16:24-26). What is interesting about Jesus's call to take up our crosses and follow Him is that the Lord challenged us before He went to the cross, not after He had overcome and been resurrected. It is hard to be excluded from friendships or be discriminated against because of our faith as we all long to be accepted and rejection of any kind hurts.

To follow Jesus means that we have to go through suffering to reach His glory (2 Thessalonians 1:5-10).[24] Suffering and glory, tribulation and entering the Kingdom of God are inseparable from one another in our pursuit of salvation. When the Lord Jesus comes again, it will be in His glory and His glory will be manifest through us who believe and follow Him.[25]

When did salvation begin?

Salvation began before the beginning of time as God predestined us to be part of His family before the foundation of the world (Ephesians 1:4-5). Salvation through Jesus our Lord is dependent on the plan of God before He created the world.[26] As Philip Graham Ryken rightly points out, the doctrine of election is a difficult doctrine because

24. John Stott. *The Bible Speaks Today: The message of 1 &2 Thessalonians,* pp. 119. InterVarsity Press, UK, revised edition 2021.
25. Ibid., pp. 119-127.
26. Philip Graham Ryken. *The Bible Speaks Today: The message of salvation.* "Before the foundation of the world," p. 65. InterVarsity Press, Leicester, UK, 2001.

it shows the sovereignty of God and that salvation ultimately depends upon God.[27] Indeed, the doctrine of election forms the five points of Calvinism which are the total depravity of mankind, unconditional election of the saints, limited atonement, irresistible grace and the perseverance of the saints.[28] The election of the saints by God is a theme that runs through the Bible and can be seen most vividly in the story of Cain and Abel, the story of the promised son Isaac over his older brother Ishmael, and in the selection of Jacob, who God loved, over Esau, who God hated.

It is by the grace of God that we are saved for eternal glory.[29] So why should we spread the gospel if God has already decided who is going to be saved? The bigger question is how will the elect know if they are saved if they had not first heard the word of God (Romans 10:14)? Therefore, it is by preaching the word and testifying to the truth of the gospel that unbelievers will come to believe in Jesus and to call upon His name and be saved. So, our faith comes through hearing the gospel and believing in the truth of that gospel (Romans 10:17).

---

27. Ibid., p. 69.

28. Edwin H. Palmer. *The Five Points of Calvinism: A Study Guide.* Baker Publishing Group, Grand Rapids, Michigan, USA, 1972. (New edition published 2012.)

29. Philip Graham Ryken, *The Bible Speaks Today: The Message of Salvation.* Part 2: "Saved by grace," pp. 61-146. InterVarsity Press, Leicester, UK, 2001.

Gospel and salvation

We are encouraged to crave the teaching of the gospel in order to grow to maturity as believers in Christ (1 Peter 2:2). We are called to proclaim the gospel and to testify about our salvation as we have been rescued from the darkness of unbelief into the light of our salvation (1 Peter 2:9). By standing on the word of God, we strengthen our belief and salvation enabling God to be our stronghold and fortress (Psalm 62:2). The word of God will sustain us through the daily challenges of life (Psalm 68:19-20). We are called to make disciples of all nations, baptising them into the Kingdom of God the Father, Jesus the Son and the Holy Spirit (Matthew 28:19). Never underestimate the power of the word of God to fulfil all that God has planned for it. Be aware that salvation comes through the Jews (John 4:22).

Prayer

Dear Heavenly Father, thank you that you have chosen us for salvation into your family and for eternal life that we may be with you in heaven. Thank you for sending your Holy Spirit to guide us into all truth as we work out our salvation in fear and trembling. Thank you, Father, for your faithfulness that we may call you Father and to know that you are an ever-present help in times of trouble, that you are our rock, our fortress and our deliverer. In Jesus's name we pray.

3.

Forgiveness

The need for forgiveness

God demands and expects perfection from mankind and it is clear to all of us that we all fall way below perfection. We all have things in our lives that we are ashamed of and wish we hadn't done or things said in anger that we wish we hadn't said. God keeps a record of our words and we will be either condemned by what we have said or set free by our words (Matthew 12:37). We all have an appointment to come before the throne of God to provide an account of what we have done during our lives on the earth whether good or evil (2 Corinthians 5:10). We will be rewarded according to our deeds in this life.

Part of the judgement will be on how we have used the talents that God has given us and whether we have used those talents for good or for evil (Matthew 25:14-30). If we bury our talents then God will take them away and give them to someone else and so there is a need to keep using the natural gifts that God has given us. There are several things that we need to understand from the parable of the talents. Firstly, we don't all have the same talents or skill sets and some people are very talented while others struggle to find their place in God's order of things. What we do with the talents God has given us is important; in other words, each one of us has an important contribution to make in this life and however small that contribution appears in our eyes, it will not be overlooked by God. As noted above, we will be held accountable for our actions and it is clear from the parable of the talents that God is concerned with our attitude and character and our response to who God is.

How God sees our sins

God is fully aware of our sins and sees them very clearly; nothing goes unnoticed by God (Isaiah 1:18), yet God wants to take away our sins. However, the choice is ours as to whether we want our sins to be taken away or whether we prefer to remain with our sins and reject God's forgiveness. There is nowhere to hide from God even when faced with the day of God's anger (Revelation 6:15-17, Job 34:21-23). We have all gone astray and turned to our own devices and want to take control of our lives outside of God (Isaiah 53:6). Every one of us has sinned against God and comes short of the requirements of God's glory (Romans 3:23) and our sins fall into two categories—the sins we wilfully do, knowing that what we are doing is wrong and the sins we carry out without knowing they are wrong. All who sin deserve God's judgement and death but God has offered us redemption and eternal life through his son Jesus Christ (Romans 6:23).

God blots out and removes our sins and does not remember them anymore; he chooses to forget our sins (Isaiah 43:25; Jeremiah 31:34). God has removed our sins as far as possible away from us (Psalm 103:12). When we consider the distance between the east and the west, we naturally think of the earth but we should be thinking in terms of the cosmos. God in his mercy casts our sins into the deepest depths of the ocean where they cannot be found (Micah 7:18-19). Jesus forgives our sins, regardless of how many we have to be forgiven, and, despite how evil we may have been in our lives, God's forgiveness is forever (Luke 7:47-50). The removal of our sins has a major impact on what we may expect when we stand before God's great throne to give an account of our lives. The only ground to stand before God on judgement day is our belief in our Lord and Saviour Jesus Christ; there is no other way that man can come before God (John 14:6).

God's forgiveness is a gift

We are challenged to seek God while he may still be found; we are called to turn from our wicked ways and to return to God, and then God will provide a pardon for our sins and no longer count them against us (Isaiah 55:6-7). God is ready to forgive us our sins if we confess to him the wrongdoings we have undertaken (Psalm 86:5). Forgiveness of sins is God's prerogative (Psalm 130:4), that is why the Jewish religious leaders thought that Jesus was blaspheming when he forgave the sins of a man who was paralysed (Matthew 9:2-6).

Receiving God's forgiveness is a two-way action. In order to be forgiven, we must first forgive and God provides the ability for us to forgive others (Ephesians 4:31-32).

However, we should note that in order to receive God's forgiveness, there is a requirement for us to turn away from our old lives and repent of our sins (Acts 3:19). We are called to repent of our old selfish lives and come out of darkness into his light (Acts 2:38). If we sin, we are among the lawless, and the Bible warns us the lawlessness will be widespread towards the end of time (1 John 3:4; 2 Thessalonians 2:7). Furthermore, as far as God is concerned, we were dead in our sinfulness as we followed the way of the world (Ephesians 2:1-3). In order to receive God's forgiveness, we have to confess our sins to God and acknowledge that we have fallen short of his standards (1 John 1:9). When we confess our sins and are delivered from the consequences of our misdeeds then we are cleansed before God. Forgiveness of our sins brings a blessing from God (Romans 4:7).

In order to receive God's forgiveness, we must forgive those who have hurt us (Colossians 3:13). The hardness of our hearts and our unwillingness to forgive break our relationship with God (Matthew 5:23-24). We need to forgive those who have sinned against us even when they don't ask for our forgiveness (Matthew 18:15; Acts 7:59-60). The consequences of not forgiving those who have hurt us result in our sins, which are many, going unforgiven by God resulting in eternal damnation (Matthew 18:34-35).

God gives us the ability to forgive others (Ephesians 4:32). It is our love for God that will determine how serious we are in forgiving those who have hurt and sinned against us. There is no limit on the number of times we need to forgive others; it is open-ended. As many times that people sin against us then that is the number of times we have to forgive others (Matthew 18:21-22).

If we conceal our sins and try to hide them from God then we will not prosper until our sins come out into the open (Proverbs 28:13). Psalm 139 shows that we cannot hide from God, and this is confirmed throughout the history of mankind; from the fall of Adam and Eve where God came looking for them in the cool of the evening, to the final moments of the current earth when God's wrath is poured out upon the unrepentant mankind who ask the mountains to fall on them and hide them from God.

Our position after forgiveness

The good news is that once we accept Jesus as our saviour and ask God for forgiveness for our past lives, then we become new creations (2 Corinthians 5:17). Our old lives have died and we are 'born again' into a new life with Christ. We may not notice the change in our life immediately, but nevertheless, it is there and will become evident as we grow in Christ. Once we have given our lives to Christ and received God's forgiveness then we are slowly transformed into the likeness of Christ (2 Corinthians 3:18). Our transformation occurs by renewing our minds and by being focused on what is important to God (Romans 12:2). We are called to imitate God by walking through life by loving God and the people we meet (Ephesians 5:1). Every one of us has a deep inherent ability to give love and to be loved. The Biblical principle is that in order to receive love, we first have to give love (Romans 5:8). God revealed his love for us by reaching out to us first, and it is this principle that we are called to follow. Sometimes, we will encounter people, perhaps even from our own families, who are difficult to love, but nevertheless, we are called to overcome our prejudices and to love these very people.

It is my belief that by loving others as we love ourselves, we will shine as beacons in the world that is so devoid of love (Matthew 5:16). By making love our central goal, we will be changed into the image of Christ (Romans 8:29). By following in the footsteps of Christ, we will become more and more like our Lord in word and in deed (1 Peter 2:21). There is a cost to following Jesus, and we are called to take up our cross and follow the Lord (Matthew 16:24). It is not a popular concept in the western world, but in order to be like Christ, there are things in our lives that need to be dealt with and these can only be dealt with by being crucified out of our lives. If we want God's best for our lives, we need to acknowledge that even after being born again and filled with the Holy Spirit, there are areas of our lives that must be regularly submitted to the cross, so that we may receive the power and victory that the Christian life promises.[30]

---

30. Paul E. Billheimer. *Overcomers Through the Cross.* Kingsway Publication Limited, Eastbourne, UK, 1984.

We are called to live by faith (Galatians 2:20), not by the things that are visible and can be readily seen. Dr Paul Yonggi Cho provides a very good anecdote of what faith requires; we need a vision of a clear objective.[31] What is it that we require from God? Dr Cho asked God for a mahogany desk, a specific type of chair and a specific type of bicycle to ride (clear vision). He told his congregation that God had provided these things (faith in God's provision). Some of his congregation came to see these items and Dr Cho had to explain that God had not yet provided them but they were coming. He told his parishioners that he was pregnant with these items (belief in what is not yet visible). Ultimately, even though Dr Cho was poor and could not buy these items, he did receive each one as a gift from God. Faith often requires us to wait on God for his provision and it takes time for the articles and desires of our faith to be revealed. On a personal note, I prayed for my mum to come to faith and belief in the Lord Jesus for 30 years, and there was no indication that God had heard my prayers. Even on the day that my mum gave her life to the Lord, there was no indication that there had been any change in my mum. Keep on believing, not for the visible but for the unseen, because God is able to do more than we hope for or imagine (Ephesians 3:20). It is impossible to please God without having faith (Hebrews 11:6).

---

31. Paul Yonggi Cho. *The Fourth Dimension*. Chapter 1: "Incubation a law of faith," pp. 9-35. Logos International Press, Plainfield, New Jersey, USA, 1979.

Prayer

Dear Heavenly Father, we come into your presence to ask for forgiveness for all our wrongdoings and sins. We ask your forgiveness for the things we have wilfully done that we know were wrong in your sight. We also ask for forgiveness for the things we are unaware of that are clearly wrong and fall short of your standards of perfection. We know that if we confess our sins and wrongdoings, you will forgive us and remember our sins no more. We are very grateful for your love for us in forgiving our sins, and we ask that we may be able to forgive ourselves for the evil we have sometimes done. We ask forgiveness for the hurt we have done to others and for the evil that is in our hearts. We are thankful for the belief that we can be imitators of you, dear Lord, and that we may grow to be like you in word, in deed and in persona. Dear Lord, give us the belief and the faith to go forward with you and to be the new creation you made us to be.

In Jesus's name we pray, Amen.

4.

Grace and mercy

What are grace and mercy?

Grace is the good favour of God which inclines him to bestow benefits upon those who do not deserve these gifts.[32] Mercy is an attribute of God which persuades God to be actively compassionate towards those of us who do not deserve it, which is all mankind. As Tozer points out, grace and truth are infinite; they were there with God from the beginning of mankind and they will be there at the end.[33] God's grace has always existed, as can be seen in the lives of both Noah and Moses (Genesis 6:8 and Exodus 33:17). God gave his grace to us before the beginning of time (2 Timothy 1:9). God's grace offers salvation to everyone who is willing to accept his grace (Titus 2:11-12). We have been saved through the grace of God, which is a gift that God freely gives to those

---

32. A. W. Tozer. *The Knowledge of the Holy*. Chapter 19: "The grace of God," pp. 100-103. STL Productions, Bromley, Kent, UK, second printing 1977.
33. A. W. Tozer. Ibid. Chapter 18: "The mercy of God," pp. 96-99.

of us who accept Jesus Christ as our Lord and Saviour (Ephesians 2:8-10). It is only through the grace of God that we can be saved and enter into God's family, by the grace shown to us through the death and resurrection of Jesus Christ.[34] It must also be noted that grace always comes through Jesus Christ. As Dietrich Bonhoeffer correctly points out, grace comes at a price; it should never be cheap. Grace without a price and without cost isn't grace at all.[35] Cheap grace enables believers to follow the desires of the world. There is no repentance of sins, no accountability, and no discipline in following Jesus and it is difficult to distinguish people under cheap grace from the world.[36] There is a cost to living under God's grace and that cost is that we must take up our cross and follow our Lord and Saviour. Are we prepared to renounce the world and the attractiveness of it and to give all to follow Christ? We are called to come out of the world and be separate (2 Corinthians 6:17). Separation from the world has always been one of the criteria that shows that the grace of God is working in the life of a Christian. As J. C. Ryle points out, the world is a great danger to the soul.[37] Separation from the world means that we are no longer

---

34. A. W. Tozer. *The Attributes of God. Volume 1: A Journey into the Father's Heart.* Chapter 6: "God's grace," pp. 100-101. Christian Publications Inc., Pennsylvania, USA, 1997.

35. Dietrich Bonhoeffer. *The Cost of Discipleship.* Chapter 1: "Costly grace," p. 3. SCM Press, London, UK, 2015 edition.

36. A. W. Tozer., ibid.

37. J. C. Ryle. *Walking with God.* Chapter 10: "The world," p. 73. Grace Publication, London, UK, 4th edition, 2003.

guided or influenced by the world's standards or what the world sees as being important for the success of man.[38]

God's mercy confronts man's inequity, suffering and guilt and without God's mercy, we would all perish under his judgement.[39] God is described as being compassionate, slow to get angry and great in mercy (Psalm 145:8). We can find God's mercy in every aspect of his work (Psalm 145:9). God also decides on those who will receive his compassion and mercy (Romans 9:15). God's mercy comes out of his great love for us (Ephesians 2:4). We receive mercy from God when we have the courage to draw near to his throne (Hebrews 4:16). God's grace and mercy are inexorably intertwined and linked together.

Our participation in God's grace

We have all received abundant grace, one blessing after another, spiritual blessing upon spiritual blessing (John 1:16). As already stated, we have been saved through the grace of God which is manifested in Jesus Christ, the Messiah, dying on a cross for our sins and iniquities (Ephesians 2:8-9). We have received every spiritual blessing available from heaven (Ephesians 1:3), but have we actually allowed the spiritual blessings and the abundant grace shown us to penetrate into our everyday living? God's grace can enable us to be filled with power and to perform signs

---

38. Ibid, pp. 77-78.

39. A. W. Tozer. *The Attributes of God. Volume 1: A Journey into the Father's Heart.* Chapter 5: "God's mercy," p. 85.

and wonders as a witness to the living God (Acts 6:8). The grace given to us is measured by God, and we can obtain more grace for our particular circumstances as we need it (Ephesians 4:7, James 4:6). Indeed, there is an abundance of grace available to us (2 Peter 1:2). We are called to give grace to others, and abound in the grace of God (2 Corinthians 8:7). In our daily living, our hearts can be strengthened to complete our tasks through the grace given to us (Hebrews 13:9). We can approach God on his throne of grace with the confidence that he will accept us because of our position in Christ (Hebrews 4:16). The reason that we approach God's throne is to receive mercy and grace in our time of need, to enable us to be overcomers of the troubles this world brings, and to be victorious as we live out our salvation as members of God's family.

Will God remove the trials and challenges we face in life? No, he won't, but he will provide the grace we need to cope with our daily battles in life (2 Corinthians 12:8-9). We are called to be faithful custodians of the grace we have been given (1 Peter 4:10). In this respect, we are called not just to be followers of Jesus, but to be disciples of Jesus, that is, to keep the commandments and words that Jesus gave us through the gospels. The call to be disciples of Christ requires that we leave our old life behind and come to be a new creation. We are called to walk by faith in Christ, and to trust God for all our requirements and needs in life (Matthew 6:25). What the world offers is very attractive; it offers success, wealth, and recognition by our fellow men, but ultimately, it is a snare to godly living and the way of Christ, and, in the end, it will lead to our destruction (Matthew 7:13-14). The contrast between entering through the narrow gate and rejecting the easy way of the world is beautifully illustrated in John Bunyan's *Pilgrim's Progress*, which is a description of the struggles that we face in life and the means through the word of God of overcoming the world.

Parables that illustrate God's grace

Jesus told two parables which illustrate what it should be like to enter into the Kingdom of God and come under his grace and mercy. The first is known as the parable of the hidden treasure and occupies just a single verse in the Bible (Matthew 13:44). The second parable follows on from the first and is known as the parable of the pearl of great price (Matthew 13:45-46). In both parables, the entry into the Kingdom of God is priceless, and in both parables, the person who finds the Kingdom of God gives up everything to own the entrance into the kingdom. When we first become Christians and give our lives to the Lord Jesus, we are excited, everything is new and we are enthusiastic to learn everything we can about our newfound lives in Christ. However, as time progresses and we return to the everyday chores of daily living, our enthusiasm for the Kingdom of God can wane and be lost. The word of God that was so alive and vibrant in our early days can be lost and as the parable of the sower illustrates, the evil one can snatch away the word of God that was sown in our hearts, or our roots are not grounded in

God and the word can shrivel and die in our hearts (Matthew 13:18-23). The cares of the world or our lust for riches can also choke the word of God and we fall away from the grace that God placed in our hearts. As Dietrich Bonhoeffer so eloquently summed up in his chapter on discipleship, "only he who believes is obedient [to the word of God, to following Christ], and only he who is obedient believes."[40]

Rich young ruler

The encounter that is perhaps at the forefront of what it means to follow Christ, and to receive God's grace and mercy, is the encounter of the rich young ruler with Jesus (Matthew 19:16-22). Again, as Bonhoeffer points out, it is a story of single-minded obedience.[41] The young man clearly believes in God, and has endeavoured to keep the law and commandments of God, but realises that there is something missing in his life. Jesus identifies the thing that is holding him back from the Kingdom of God as his wealth, which Jesus asks him to give up and follow him. This is something the young man cannot do and walks away in great misery, unhappiness and sadness. Does following Jesus require that we sell all our possessions and step out into the world in faith? The answer is only if our

---

40. Dietrich Bonhoeffer. *The Cost of Discipleship*. Chapter 2: "The call to discipleship," p. 21. SCM Press, London, UK, 2015 edition.
41. Dietrich Bonhoeffer. *The Cost of Discipleship*. Chapter 3: "Single-minded obedience," pp. 35-40.

possessions are more important to us than Jesus. It is of great interest that the disciples found the treatment of the rich young man difficult to accept, and asked who can possibly be saved and enter heaven? (Matthew 19:23-26).

God will come at some point in our lives, identify what we hold most dearly, and ask us to surrender it to him because that will be the thing that is preventing us from fully entering into his grace and mercy. This principle is clearly illustrated in the faith that Abraham showed in being willing to sacrifice Isaac to the Lord because God asked him to (Genesis 22:1-19). Are we prepared to make a similar sacrifice to follow Jesus and to surrender what is most precious in our lives to God? Anyone who makes sacrifices for God will be rewarded one hundredfold and also receive eternal life (Matthew 19:29). However, it is still a big step to make those sacrifices.

God's grace in action

Jesus alluded to the grace of God in action in a parable at the beginning of Matthew chapter 20 verses 1-16. The parable describes a landowner (Jesus) who goes out at varying stages of the day to hire workers to work in his vineyard (heaven). He starts by hiring workers early in the morning and promising to pay a single day's wages (one denarius), then, throughout the day he hires more workers until the evening and promises to pay each worker a day's wages. At the end of the day, the workers line up to receive their wages (a denarius, equivalent to a place in the Kingdom of Heaven). Unlike human business owners, Jesus starts to pay those who were hired at the end of the day first. Normally, good business practice would be to pay those who have worked all day first for they have done the longest shift. However, Jesus was true to his word; those who were hired last were paid a full day's pay. When he got to those who had worked all day, he paid them one denarius, the same wage as those who were hired last. Not surprisingly, those who were hired first were not best pleased and began to grumble. Jesus pointed out that he was paying each worker what he promised to pay them. Jesus also underlined that in the Kingdom of heaven, those who are last will be first and those who were first will be last. This is the opposite of what men and women would expect to happen on earth. I often wonder what the trade union representatives would make of this situation?

The main consideration that arises is this—what do you think would happen the next day if this landowner went out to hire workers? Would any worker wish to be hired early in the morning and work throughout the heat of the day? Would workers merely turn up at the end of the day to be hired knowing that they would be paid for a full day's work? The final point made by Jesus is that he is being good to pay each worker the same wage. The key take-home message from the passage is that God is completely fair in administering his grace and mercy. What men and women achieve in this life in terms of honour or possessions does not count in God's kingdom. Everyone in God's kingdom will be treated equally, regardless of their ability to work long hours. There is no favouritism or partiality with God (Romans 2:11).

Consequences of not accepting God's grace

God's wrath (anger) for our sins remains on all those who do not accept Jesus as their Lord and Saviour (John 3:36). God's anger remains against all ungodliness and all those who are unrighteous in his sight (Romans 1:18). God is coming to punish the inhabitants of the earth who have rejected his provision of eternal life through the grace and mercy he has shown in Jesus (Isaiah 26:21). Those who reject Jesus remain under God's judgement and they will be punished for their iniquities and sins; such people remain adversaries of God and will experience God's vengeance (Nahum 1:2). God has the ability to destroy our body and soul in hell (Matthew 10:28). This will be the fate of anyone whose name is not written in God's Book of Life (Revelation 20:15). The anger of God will be poured out on all those who are rebellious and who have rejected God's provision of eternal life through his son Jesus Christ (Ephesians 5:6). God will punish the ungodly and those deemed lacking in righteousness (2 Peter 2:9). However, if we confess our shortcomings, failures and sins then God will cleanse us from our transgressions and iniquities (1 John 1:9). Therefore, do not go on sinning and evoking God's anger after becoming a Christian, because God will judge his children, and it is frightening to fall into the hands of the living God (Hebrews 10:26-31). The saddest outcome of all is that most men and women prefer to remain in their iniquities, and when God pours out his anger, they will call upon the rocks to fall upon them to hide them from God's anger (Revelation 6:16).

The final word on God's grace and mercy

In God's grace and mercy, all our fears are put to rest. It is a mystery that God knows each and every one of us better than we know ourselves. God has been placed in a place of authority over the world we live in (Psalm 8:4-8). God notices us in a crowd of people, regardless of how large that crowd is; there is no place we can go where God's love will fail to find us; no place we can hide that God doesn't see us; God discerns our going out and our staying at home; darkness doesn't hide us from God; there is no place we can fall in our lives that God's love cannot catch us and lift us back to where we belong; when we are awake, God is with us, and he is there while we sleep and rest (Psalm 139). Nothing can separate us from the love of God (Romans 8:38-39).

Prayer

Dear Heavenly Father, I am so grateful for the grace and mercy you show to me in my life every day. Thank you that you care for me and watch over me. Thank you that you know when I go out and when I stay in. Thank you that you notice me in a crowd and are always with me when I am happy or sad, depressed or ecstatic, lonely or among friends and family. Thank you that you are the constant in my life. Lord Jesus, we acknowledge that we are able to live in God's grace and mercy because of what you sacrificed on the cross for us. We are grateful that your steadfast love never ceases and your mercies never come to an end. Thank you that your love for us is renewed every day and we have a hope and a future because of you.

In Jesus's name we pray, Amen

5.

God's favour

GOD HAS SHOWN HIS favour to man from the beginning of time as we were predestined before the creation of the world (Ephesians 1:4). We did not choose Jesus but he chose us to go and bear fruit for his kingdom (John 15:16). We have been called and predestined to carry out his purposes on the earth (Romans 8:28-30). God has chosen us from the beginning so that we may be saved and sanctified so that we can believe in Jesus as our Lord and Saviour (2 Thessalonians 2:13). The good news is that we have been chosen according to God's foreknowledge to be part of his family and to share in the inheritance of the saints for eternity (1 Peter 1:2).

Finding favour in God's eyes

In the account of the creation of the world, God created Adam and Eve in His own image, and he blessed them (Genesis 1:27-28). Moving forward to Abel, the

Lord accepted Abel's offering but he rejected Cain's (Genesis 4:4). Among all the rebellious people and wickedness on the earth, Noah found favour in the Lord's eyes (Genesis 6:8), and Noah and his family were saved from the destruction that God heaped on mankind for their wickedness. While Joseph was wrongfully imprisoned in Egypt, he was shown favour by God (Genesis 39:21). Moses found favour in God's eyes as he was tasked to bring Israel out of Egypt (Exodus 33:12). The people of Israel were shown God's favour, and God caused his face to shine upon them (Numbers 6:25). Samuel, as a boy, grew in stature and in favour with both the Lord and men (1 Samuel 2:26). Even when things were not going well for Israel, God was gracious to them and showed them his favour and compassion on account of the covenant he had made with Abraham (2 Kings 13:23). Mary, the mother of our Lord Jesus, found favour with God when she was chosen to be the mother of his son (Luke 1:30). Not surprisingly, Jesus, when he was on the earth himself, kept increasing in wisdom, stature, and with God's favour (Luke 2:52).

We can call upon God to bless us and make his face to shine upon us (Psalm 67). If we walk according to the commands and statures of God, then we can expect him to bless us. However excited we may be now, or however sad, despondent and depressed we are, praising God and turning to him for help is the starting point of finding favour with God, and returning to the centre of his blessing. Remembering what God has done for us in the past can strengthen us in times when God seems far from us.

There are many times when we will need to call upon the Lord to make his face shine upon us so that we may bring glory to his name (Psalm 31:16; Psalm 67:1; Psalm 80:3; Psalm 119:135). Often, we call on God to show us favour so that we can come back to the narrow path that leads to eternal life, from which it is so easy to stray.

Hindrances to receiving God's favour

The obvious hindrance to receiving God's favour and blessing is that we continue to deliberately sin after we are saved (Hebrews 10:26). Becoming a Christian and being forgiven for our sins does not give us the license to continue sinning. We are asked to dispose of our old self and the bad habits we knew before we turned to Christ (2 Corinthians 5:17). The sins we should leave behind when we become Christians are listed as adultery, sexual immorality, and idolatry; that is considering anything more important than God to the point that it becomes the centre of our desires and our ambition. Idolatry can be an obsession with a football team, with our house, our family, or our career to the point of excluding all other things. Hatred of others is a sin that could lead to dark thoughts, and replace the position that God should have in our lives. Jealousy, anger, selfish ambition, heresy, envy of others, murder, and drunkenness all fall into the sphere of works of the flesh (Galatians 5:19-21). We are warned that people who have these traits will not enter into the Kingdom of God, nor will they receive God's favour.

Remaining in God's favour

William Law hit the nail on the head when he stated that people fall short of pleasing God and remaining in his favour because they simply don't try or don't desire to be godly, humble, love others and set aside time to grow in God.[42] To continue to please God and find favour with him, we must desire to do so above all else. Throughout his book *A Serious Call to a Devout and Holy Life*, William Law (1686-1761), stresses over and over that the missing ingredient in failing to continue in God's favour is a lack of desire.[43]

However, what does God desire of us to continue in his favour? God requires us to act fairly in all our dealings, to be merciful toward anyone who offends us and to walk humbly with our God (Micah 6:8). Humility is defined as the fear of God (Proverbs 22:4) and its reward as honour, riches and life. God guides those who are humble in what is correct and teaches us his ways (Psalm 25:9). The importance of being humble is a theme that is repeated throughout the Bible. We are called to clothe ourselves with compassion, kindness, humility, gentleness and patience (Colossians 3:12). Be humble, gentle and patient bearing each other in love (Ephesians 4:2). How many times in our lives would we have liked people to be patient and kind towards us, and instead, we

---

42. William Law. *A Serious Call to a Devout and Holy Life*. Chapter 2: "An enquiry into the reason why most Christians fall so far short of the holiness and devotion to Christianity," p. 15. Hodder and Stoughton, London, UK, 1987.

43. Ibid.

have received harshness and judgement? Don't be vain or conceited but value the opinions of others more highly than our own (Philippians 2:3). How different the world would be if we learnt to listen to other people's views and consider that they are putting forward valued points of view. We are called to live in harmony with one another and we should be willing to befriend people from all walks of life, even those who we would normally consider below our intellectual or social standing (Romans 12:16). In this respect, Christianity should stand out from the world and all other charities and social groups; unfortunately, Christians so often are just a mirror image of the world. Finally, if we humble ourselves before God, he will lift us up at the proper time to stand above our circumstances (James 4:10).

Anger as a factor that displeases God

Anger has always been a problem in our world and there are good statistics suggesting that it is becoming an increasing problem in the world we live in. Some 84% of people surveyed said Americans are angrier today compared with a generation ago, according to the latest NPR-IBM Watson Health poll. When asked about their own feelings, 42% of those polled said they were angrier in the past year than they had been further back in time. The poll found that 29% of people said they were often angry when checking the news. Another 42% said the news sometimes made them angry.[44] In 2019, research from the American Automobile Association revealed that 80% of drivers had expressed anger or aggression in the previous 30 days.[45] The survey found that road rage was directly responsible for 1,800 injuries and 30 murders each year. Over a 7-year period, road rage was directly responsible for 200 deaths and 12,000 injuries in the United States of America. Furthermore, road rage deaths had increased 5-fold over a 10-year period and they are still increasing year on year.

Jesus warned that anyone who is angry with his brother or sister without good cause was in danger of God's displeasure and judgement (Matthew 5:22). As Bonhoeffer identified, anger is an attack on the person we are angry with, and aims at that person's destruction.[46] Every angry word we utter shows contempt for the person we are angry with and places our own priorities above the person we are angry with. Bonhoeffer went as far as stating that when we swear at, publicly slander, or insult a person, we are, in effect, committing murder. When we hurt, damage or disgrace a person, then we erect a barrier between God and ourselves.

---

44. Scott Hensley. "Poll: Americans Say We're Angrier Than a Generation Ago." June 26, 2019. https://www.npr.org/sections/health-shots/2019/06/26/735757156/poll-americans-say-were-angrier-than-a-generation-ago

45. Robert Muñoz. "Seeing Red: 87 Road Rage Statistics That Will Make Your Blood Boil (2020-2021)." March 13, 2022. https://sensiblemotive.com/road-rage-statistics/

46. Dietrich Bonhoeffer. *The Cost of Discipleship*. Chapter 9: "The Brother," pp. 79-82.

God's word allows us to be angry, but points out that we should not sin when we are angry, and that we should never let the sun go down on our anger (Ephesians 4:26). There is righteous anger which is a form of anger when we see injustice or hurt meted out against an innocent person; for example, when we see the atrocities of war, such as children who have taken refuge being targeted indiscriminately by invading forces. Indeed, Jesus showed anger against those who were misusing God's temple in Jerusalem for their own personal, greedy gain (Matthew 21:12-13; John 2:13-16). Also, Jesus rebuked his disciples for not allowing children and infants to come to him (Mark 10:13-16).

Ingredients needed for favour with God

A key component in our walk with God is to seek wisdom because through wisdom, we will find favour with the Lord (Proverbs 8:35). During my life, I have met many very clever people, but many of them lack common sense, and even fewer have obtained wisdom. The Bible's guidance for the young is that if they hold onto mercy and truth, then they can find favour, great esteem and a good name before God (Proverbs 3:3-4). Ultimately, a good man or woman will find favour with the Lord (Proverbs 12:2).

God's favour borne out in practice

An example of God's favour is in the account of the prophet Elijah during the reign of King Ahab of Israel. During Ahab's reign, Israel disregarded God's commandments and followed after other gods in the form of Baal and Asherah (1 Kings 18:18). Under God's instruction, Elijah prophesied a drought over Israel which lasted 3 years. After 3 years, Elijah gathered together the 450 prophets of Baal and the four hundred prophets of Asherah, as well as the whole of Israel, for a showdown. Elijah proposed that the two opposing sides set up a sacrifice and the God who sent down fire on the burnt offering would be the one true God (1 Kings 18:23-38). Needless to say, the false prophets of Baal and Asherah had no success but the living God sent down fire to prove that he was the one true God (1 Kings 18:38). The false prophets were put to death and it was a huge triumph for Elijah. After such success, Elijah may have expected promotion to head prophet, together with all the accolades that would be associated with such a promotion.

However, Ahab's wife, Jezebel, the queen of Israel, was outraged and planned to send around some soldiers to discuss Elijah's early retirement plan, which would be permanent. Not surprisingly, Elijah ran away and was so depressed that he wanted to die (1 Kings 19:4). It is a common human reaction to be depressed when things don't work out the way we want them to, especially at work. Part of the problem here is, who do we measure ourselves against? Elijah's complaint was that he was no better than his father. We don't know if Elijah's father was a good role model, and we should always measure ourselves by our own standards and try to gain a perspective on what we have achieved. Nowhere in the Bible do we see Elijah's father causing fire to come down from heaven or praying into existence a drought that lasted 3 years.

God's favour is shown that while Elijah is sleeping in the desert, God sends him an angel to bring him water and food (1 Kings 19:7-8). The moral at this point is that we can't run away from our troubles; we are going to take them with us. At some point, we will have to face whatever catastrophe that has occurred in our lives.

Elijah continues on his journey for 40 days and 40 nights until he reaches Mount Horeb (1 Kings 19:9). Only when he reaches Horeb does Elijah come before God. As a rule, when we face trouble in our lives, we should turn to God, ask for his help, and seek his wisdom and guidance in our situation. We should not wait 40 days before coming before God. Then God's first question to Elijah is "What are you doing here?" It is a question that God may often ask of us when our faith fails us in difficult times. After asking Elijah the question, God passes before Elijah in a small voice, which indicates that we have to find a quiet place and be calm to listen to what has to say when we need his help. God then provides the solution to Elijah's problem, which shows God's favour for those who follow him and are loyal to his calling. It wasn't Elijah's life that was on the line but those of his enemies who were ultimately removed by God. It is always good to know that God wasn't fazed by Elijah's predicament, and, despite his surprise at finding Elijah on Mount Horeb, God listened to what Elijah had to say.

There are many more instances of God showing his favour. For example, God showed his favour to Abel above Cain, to Noah and his family by saving them from the flood, to Abraham by making him the father of many nations, to Jacob over Esau, to Joseph in Egypt, to Moses when leading Israel, to David, despite him being an adulterer and a murderer, and the list goes on. However, one account from 2 Kings 6:8-23 is worth mentioning in a little more detail. Syria was at war with Israel, but Elisha kept warning the Israelites which areas to avoid. Not surprisingly, the Syrians got frustrated by this and sent a large army to surround the city where Elisha was in order to capture him. When Elisha's servant came out early in the morning, he was horrified to see this vast army and was perturbed that there appeared no way of escape, which is often the case when we look at the earthly situation. Elisha was able to see that those God sent to protect the city from the Syrians far outnumbered the vast army that surrounded them. Elisha had to pray for his servant's eyes to be opened so that he may see that the mountain was covered with horses and chariots of fire. Elisha, who was one man, was able to send blindness on the Syrian army and lead them into captivity. When we continue to look to God regardless of how terrible the circumstances appear, then the possibilities for success are endless.

Prayer

Dear Heavenly Father, thank you that when we stay true to our calling as Christians, we have your favour in our lives. It is good to know that you are our God and you are the same yesterday, today and forever, and you are a God who was, and is and is to come. We acknowledge that nothing ever phases you, our Lord and Saviour, and we can rely on your favour in our good times and when our circumstances change for the worse. Teach us, dear Lord, to always look to you each morning, and to know that the steadfast love of the Lord never changes; your blessings are endless. Thank you, Father, that you are an ever-present help in times of trouble and that we can rely upon you to deliver us from the evil one. Help us to grow in favour before you and to develop a deeper love for you and a greater understanding of your purposes. Help us to always see beyond the immediate joys and difficulties and open our eyes to see that those who are for us are greater than those who are against us.

In Jesus's name we pray, Amen

6.

Holiness

As I BEGIN THIS chapter on holiness, I am aware that
there are several excellent books written on this theme.
These books include but are not limited to J. C. Ryle, *Holiness;*[47] John White, *The Path to Holiness: A Guide for Sinners;*[48] and David Wilkinson, *A Holiness of the Heart.*[49] In
addition to these books on holiness, there is an excellent
chapter by A. W. Tozer in the *Attributes of God* volume
one.[50] Each of the authors I list above struggles with a
definition of holiness. Tozer describes it as being pure but
then states that being pure doesn't go far enough.[51] White
describes holiness in negative terms as being the absence

---

47. J. C. Ryle. *Holiness.* Evangelical Press, Welwyn, England, 1979. (Originally published in 1879.)

48. John White. *The Pathway of Holiness: A Guide for Sinners.* Eagle, Inter Publishing Services, Guildford, England, 1996.

49. David Wilkinson. *A Holiness of the Heart.* Monarch Books, London, England, 2000.

50. A. W. Tozer. *The Attributes of God. Volume 1.* Chapter 9: "God's holiness." Christian Publications Inc., Camp Hill, PA, USA, 1997.

51. Ibid., p. 159.

of sin in our lives; Christian perfection.[52] J. C. Ryle states that true practical holiness is a hard definition to make, and is concerned that he will give a defective view of holiness.[53] However, Ryle settles on the definition that holiness is being of one mind with God. Wilkinson states that he misunderstood holiness and went on a personal journey of misconceptions regarding holiness.[54] All authors agree that to be holy is to be like God. However, God is infinite, omnipotent, omnipresent and perfect, to list but a few attributes of God. For a fuller list, see Tozer's books on the attributes of God, both volume one and volume two. *The New Bible Dictionary* defines holiness in terms of something that is applied in the highest sense to God and the outshining of all God is.[55] *The New Bible Dictionary* also states that holiness is designated of places and seasons, and to people and to the whole nation of Israel, to various articles within the Temple and the Tabernacle, and, of course, to Christians. Perhaps the best definition of holiness is that God is light and in Him, there is no darkness at all (1 John 1:5). When we consider and focus on the reality that God is light, then we come to realise the darkness, sin and iniquity in the life of every believer must be dealt with and that is why Jesus had to come to die on the cross for our sins and to reconcile us to God.

---

52. John White, ibid., p. 6.
53. J. C. Ryle, ibid., p. 34.
54. David Wilkinson, ibid., pp. 12-19.
55. *The New Bible Dictionary.* Inter Varsity Press, London, UK, 1974.

Holy God

The seraphim around the throne of God declare that God is holy (Isaiah 6:3; Revelation 4:8). God's name is holy and we are warned very severely not to take the Lord's name in vain or blaspheme his name. (Isaiah 57:15; Deuteronomy 5:11) Whenever men encountered the living God in his glory, they fell down on their knees before him in fear of being destroyed (Isaiah 6:5; Ezekiel 1:28; Revelation 1:17). So brilliant is the glory of God that mortal men or women cannot see it and live. God refers to himself as the 'Holy One, Israel's creator' (Isaiah 43:15). God is incomparable, and there is no one holy like our God (1 Samuel 2:2). All there is regarding God is holy and beyond our comprehension (Psalm 77:13; Isaiah 40:25). Men and women are not to blaspheme God's holy name, or say anything derogatory about his name (Leviticus 22:32). Everything that surrounds God is holy including his throne, his hill and mountain, his habitation, his temple and his righteousness (Psalm 11:4; Psalm 15:1; Psalm 47:8; Psalm 48:1; Habakkuk 2:20; Zechariah 2:13).

When Moses first encountered God in the desert, he was told to take off his shoes because he was standing on holy ground (Exodus 3:5). I doubt that the ground was holy before God arrived and it is unlikely that the ground remained holy for very long after God left. There are no words to describe God. When asked, God refers to himself as I AM WHO I AM, and when pushed on who Moses should tell the Israelites sent him, God's reply was "I AM sent you" (Exodus 3:14). God's name is often translated into English as Yahweh, which means to exist or to be. Some translations refer to Yahweh as Jehovah.[56] It is also worth noting that the Israelites do not utter the name of God for fear of blaspheming. If only Christians had the same reverence for the name of God. In modern Christian circles, there is too much familiarity with God, and we don't hold God in the esteem that is due to his holy name, or to God per se. There is no longer the awe of encountering or coming into the presence of the living God that is so evident in earlier Christian generations.

Names for God

The word translated as "glory" from New Testament Greek is *doxa*, which may be defined as esteem, and is related to the thanksgiving, praise and reverence we should provide to God for who he is. Glorifying God is part of our personal relationship with God, and developing our understanding of who God is.[57] Today, the names for God are little more than labels for a predominant or preeminent being. God's names fail to convey the true character of God, what God is like, or God's relationship to each one of us. However, in the Bible, the names given to God provide insight into who the living God truly is, and God's names carry special significance for his people.[58]

---

56. "Names of God" in the Bible.org: https://bible.org/article/names-god#. Accessed April 2022.
57. Ibid.
58. Ibid.

Associated with the name Yahweh are a number of additional suffixes, such as Yahweh/Jehovah Jireh, meaning the Lord will provide, indicating that God's provision is sufficient for us in our everyday needs (Genesis 22:14).

Elohim is a name that could be translated as 'the strong one'; it is used to denote God's sovereignty and creativity and his mighty work on behalf of his people (Genesis 1:1; Deuteronomy 5:23 and 8:15; Psalm 68:7; Isaiah 45:18 and 54:5; Jeremiah 32:27).[59] Jehovah Nissi, God is my banner, relates to God putting his protection over us and the means of our victories in life (Exodus 17:15); God is our peace (Judges 6:24); God is the Lord of hosts, and is the commander of the heavenly armies (I Samuel 1:3 and 17:45); God as the means of our sanctification (Exodus 31:13); God is our righteousness, the door by which we may enter into his kingdom (Jeremiah 23:6); God is here, showing God's personal presence in the world and among his people (Ezekiel 48:35; God is my shepherd, who cares for his beloved people (Psalm 23:1).[60] Indeed, Jesus referred to himself as the true shepherd of the sheep, and as the door for the sheep to enter into God's kingdom, and at the end of the discourse, Jesus stated that he and God are the same person (John 10:1-30).

Other names for God include the most high God (Genesis 14:19; Daniel 7:18) and the everlasting God, which emphasises God's infinitude (Genesis 16:13). In the New Testament Greek Theos, the only true, unique, transcendent God is the most common name for God

---

59. Ibid.
60. Ibid.

(Matthew 23:9; Romans 3:30; John 17:3; Acts 17:24; John 3:16).[61] Theos is also used when referring to Jesus as God (John 1:1; and 1:18 and 20:28). Of course, there is the most famous "Abba" Father (Romans 8:15). Also, there is the frequent use of the word 'Lord' in the New Testament, showing God's authority and supremacy.

In overview, the many names for God in the Bible provide us with a good starting point when considering who God is and his holiness.

Called to be holy

God calls us to be holy because he is holy (1 Peter 1:16; 1 Thessalonians 4:7). God craves for us to be like he is; that is the ultimate journey of every Christian. We know that when Jesus returns to the earth, we will be like him (1 John 3:2). In other words, we are unable to truly grasp what God is like, and all our images or imaginations of who God is fall far short of the reality of God. The importance of holiness is emphasized through the fact that without being holy, we are unable to see God (Hebrews 12:14).

For men and women, there are three stages of holiness. Firstly, we were made holy when we accepted Jesus as our Lord and Saviour (Hebrews 10:10). This type of holiness is referred to as positional holiness; we are holy because God says we are holy. As J. C. Ryle points out in his book on holiness, those who want to understand what

____

61. Ibid.

it means to be holy must first examine and understand the vast concept of sin.[62] The acts of a sinful nature are listed in Mark 7:20-23; 1 Corinthians 6:9-10 and Galatians 5:19-21 to name but a few places.

The second stage of holiness is progressive holiness; God is making us holy as we learn more about him and desire to be more like him (Hebrews 10:14). God, who has begun to work on our hearts and minds, to transform us into the likeness of His son Jesus, will complete the work (Philippians 1:6). It is reassuring to know that we are the work of God, and, in this present life, we are very much work in progress. Not surprisingly, the Bible has most to say about progressive holiness because that is where we are at the moment. We are called to mirror the likeness of God (Romans 8:29; 2 Corinthians 3:18), and to present our bodies in a manner that reflects our holiness and is therefore pleasing to God (Romans 12:1-2). There are days when we may look at ourselves and think, what on earth is God doing with me? Yet, Ephesians 1:4 reassures us that God chose us before the creation of the world to be grafted into His family, and more importantly to be holy and blameless before Him. Our role in the work that God is carrying out in our lives is to be imitators of God; in other words, to endeavour to be like God, as much as our minds are able to grasp what God is truly like (Ephesians 5:1).

The third and final stage of holiness is complete holiness; when Christ returns, we will be like him (1 John 3:2).

---

62. J. C. Ryle. *Holiness*. Chapter 1: "Sin," p. 1-14. Evangelical Press, Welwyn, England, 1979. (originally published in 1879.)

We will be able to stand in the presence of God, we will be his people and he will be our God (Revelation 21:3). We will be able to see the face of God and live (Revelation 22:4). This is an important revelation because God told Moses that no one could see his face and live (Exodus 33:20), therefore, only those who are holy can see the face of God and live. The seraphim are creatures that stand around the throne of God in heaven. They have six wings, and two of those wings cover their faces because they cannot see the face of God and live (Isaiah 6:2-3). Isaiah is undone by his unclean lips and speech. Jesus warned us that we will be judged for every careless word we have spoken (Matthew 12:36). Isaiah's lips are made clean by a seraph who touches his lips with a live coal taken from the altar of God (Isaiah 6:6-7). The coal would have left painful blisters on Isaiah's lips showing that there is a cost to being made clean before God.

Working out our belief in holiness

Before we can enter the Kingdom of God, we have to repent and turn our back completely on our old life. As John White states, pain, real pain is part of the process of repentance.[63] As Jesus pointed out in Luke 13:3, unless we repent, we will all perish. As J. C. Ryle surmises, this is a hard saying for many.[64] However, Ryle goes on to show

---

63. John White, ibid., p. 72.
64. J. C. Ryle. *Old Paths*. Chapter 16: "Repentance," pp. 403-435. Banner of Truth Trust, Edinburgh, Scotland, 1999.

that the words of Christ were words of love and came from the person who left heaven to come to earth and die for our sins. The definition of repentance given by Ryle is that we change our hearts in relation to sin. We naturally orientate towards sin, which, in reality, is a rejection of God's commandments and precepts, and go along in life with our own selfish way and a total disregard for others. The Bible calls this attitude lawlessness, and we see it often in everyday life, and in all manner of guises. For example, we see a society without any morals and ethics, the outcome being an increase in violence and immorality, a complete loss of safe and decent living, a disrespect towards God, towards parents, and towards anyone in authority; the earth is corrupt before God.[65]

True repentance involves recognising what our sins are, being touched by how evil we have been in the past, confessing our sins to God, asking for forgiveness for our sins, and breaking with the past to a new direction with God (Acts 2:37-38).[66]

We return to the pivotal truth that if any man is in Christ, he is a new creation and the old sinful life is dead (2 Corinthians 5:17). We are made new creatures by a process which involves receiving the Holy Spirit (Acts 2:38-39), who will come into our lives to teach us all the things of God (John 14:25-26).[67]

---

65. "Lawlessness in society." *Reformed Witness Hour.* Sept. 26, 2010. Ac. April 2022. https://reformedwitnesshour.org/broadcast/lawlessness-in-society
66. J. C. Ryle, ibid., p. 403-435.
67. Charles Spurgeon. *Christ's Glorious Achievements: What Jesus Has Done for You.* Chapter 4: "Christ the maker of all things new." Christian Focus Publications, Ross-shire, UK, 2003.

In reality, when revival comes into our hearts and the hearts of our communities, there is a tangible change in life. For example, in the great Welsh revival at the beginning of the 20th century, there were stories of public houses being emptied as the Holy Spirit came upon the occupants with power. People who had for many years been drunkards could no longer face drinking alcoholic beverages. Churches that for many years had been in decline were filled with people seeking God. There was a fierce longing for a deeper personal relationship with God. Fewer crimes were committed in the communities and there was a deep-seated turning away from lawlessness. The streets echoed with hymns rather than drunkards' songs. Bridges and street walls, instead of being covered with obscene graffiti, were covered with Bible verses. Men who had gambled or drunk away their salaries now brought their salaries home to their wives and children, resulting in an improvement in family life.[68]

Notice that it is the Holy Spirit working in us that makes us new creations. We do not become new creations by our own efforts, but rather by who we are in Christ, and by the working of the Holy Spirit in us that works to change our perspectives of life.[69]

---

68. "The Welsh Revival" by Roy Jenkins. Accessed April 2022. BBC.co.uk/religion/religions/Christianity/history/Welshrevival
69. Charles Spurgeon, ibid.

All things for good

If we are called according to God's purpose, then everything is working for our good (Romans 8:28). As we grow in holiness, then God is at work in us regardless of our circumstances, the challenges we face, or the victories we achieve. We are called to come out of the world and be separated from the objectives, reality and direction in which worldly obsessions would take us (2 Corinthians 6:17). Our hearts and desires will only become spiritual when they are renewed by the Holy Spirit and Christ dwells in our hearts.[70] As J. C. Ryle questioned, have we overcome the world or are we overcome by it? Are we separate from the world's goals, desires and objectives or are we still a part of it?[71] Once we have come out of the world in the sense that we are no longer driven by worldly desires of success and focus on what Christ calls important, then we are on the correct narrow way that leads to holiness and eternal life.

However, we return to the fact that it is God that is working in us to slowly change us into the likeness of his son Jesus (Philippians 1:6). Along our journey to holiness, we will find that our spirits are poor but we will find a place in God's kingdom; we will have times when things don't appear to be going to plan and we mourn for a better life; we will find meekness; we will be hungry and thirsty for God's righteousness and find our fulfilment in spiritual pursuits; we will learn to be merciful, makers of

70. J. C. Ryle. *Walking with God.* Chapter 10: "The world," pp. 73-79.
71. Ibid.

peace, becoming pure in heart; we can expect to be persecuted at times in our lives but ultimately, we will be able to see God and inherit a place in God's kingdom (Matthew 5:3-10). Much of our discomfort and misery in our faith is caused by not realising who we are in Christ. We are children of God and when Christ returns, we shall be like him (1 John 3:2). All who believe in Christ are children of God (John 1:12-13). That is our position now, so think about our position as children of God for a moment. The Bible isn't concerned very much with those who reject Christ other than warning them of their ultimate fate, but the word of God, especially the New Testament, has much to say about what it means to be children of God.[72] Once we grasp that we are children of God and we are destined for heaven, we will realise that we are holy because God calls us holy; it is not something that we need to strive for or chase after.[73] Therefore, we will have a desire to follow God's ways to have a pure heart so that we can see God more clearly (1 John 3:3). The key question is, do we want God to change us into the likeness of his son? If the answer is yes, then will we allow God the access he needs to continue his good work within us? This can be an issue for us in the modern western world, where Jesus may find that we are neither hot nor cold; we are lukewarm in our commitment to God, and our priorities are far from being centred on the work of God. There is much at stake for those who are only nominal in

---

72. Martyn Lloyd-Jones. *Life in Christ. Volume 3: Children of God*, studies in 1 John, pp. 21-48. Crossway Books, Nottingham, England, 1993.
73. Ibid., pp. 41-43.

their faith. Jesus stands at the door of our hearts waiting for the invitation to enter fully into our lives (Revelation 3:19-20). The reward for opening the door of our hearts to Jesus is the opportunity to sit on the throne of God with him (Revelation 3:21). This is an opportunity to share in the Government of God, something to cherish and not pass up lightly. God expects from born-again Christians an excellency that is above the ordinary to an exact moral purity, not conforming to the standards of this world but being transformed into the likeness of Jesus.[74] It is good to know that Christ is in heaven praying for the sanctification of those who love him and that we will eventually be where he is (John 17:17 and 24).

---

74. Lewis Bayly. *The Practice of Piety*, pp. 78-81.

Prayer

Dear Heavenly Father, forgive us for our sins and the many times we have fallen short of your desires for our lives. Change our hearts and minds so that we may clearly focus on your desires for our lives. We invite you into our hearts so that we may be slowly changed into the likeness of your son with heavenly goals and cravings. May each day be a new day that we may become more holy in our thoughts, words and deeds. May each day bring new opportunities to follow more closely those ideals and objectives that are close to your heart. May your will reign in our lives and thank you, Father, for never giving up on us. May your grace and mercy grow more and more in our hearts so that we can become more like you. In Jesus's name we pray, Amen.

7.

God's love for the world

What is love?

In the Old Testament, love, whether human or Godly, is the deepest expression of the closest personal relationship possible between two people or between God and man.[75] In the New Testament, the Greek word *agape* expresses the highest form of love, and builds on the Old Testament definition of a sacrificial form of love which gives everything. God's deep love for the world resulted in him sacrificing his precious son to atone for our wickedness and failure to live up to his standards of holiness (John 3:16). The second common Greek word for love in the New Testament is *phileo* and is used of intimate affection, of loving to do pleasant things and of brotherly love.[76] Indeed, there are four different words used to define love in Greek. In addition to agape and phileo,

---

75. *The New Bible Dictionary.* Inter Varsity Press, London, UK, 1974.
76. Ibid.

there is *eros* which is romantic love; erotic desire; intimacy or infatuation with another's beauty, and *storgē* which refers to familial love; affection; natural empathy for one's family, country, or team.[77]

The *Oxford Paperback Dictionary* defines love as strong feelings of affection, or strong feelings of affection linked to sexual attraction, or a great affection or interest in something.[78] However, true love goes far beyond these definitions, and into the realm of what is at the centre of mankind and the centre of the heart of God.

The next question is, what is the object of our love? I'd love a cup of coffee; I'd love a bowl of fresh fruit; I love going shopping; I love my football/cricket/basketball/sports club; I love the National Health Service; I love my job; I love it when my competitors fail; I love the countryside; I love nature; I love my partner and my children; I love my dog/cat; I love my country; I love the Lord my God. These are all expressions of love with very different meanings and implications. Yet, each saying expresses how we feel about various situations or objects of our affection. Can we and should we divide love into a number of different categories, so that we can better express what we mean and are feeling? Should some of our expressions of love fall into the category of 'like'? For example, I'd really like a cup of tea, or I'd really like to go shopping. Therefore, when talking and thinking about

---

77. https://www.biblicalarchaeology.org/daily/what-god-is-love-actually-means/
78. *Oxford Paperback Dictionary*, Oxford, England, 2001.

love, we must keep in mind the true meaning of what we are communicating.

Indeed, C. S. Lewis divided natural love into the four Greek categories; affection (agape), friendship (phileo), eros (which may also contain aspects of the other three Greek words for love), and charity (storgē/agape).[79] In many senses, Lewis's definition of the four loves overlaps the four Greek definitions of love in that there can be more than a single type of Greek definition in each of his four categories. Lewis gives the love of a mother for her baby as an example of affection. He describes this type of love as a need-love of the baby requiring milk from the mother and a gift-love as the mother freely provides milk for her baby.[80] Lewis qualifies affection, whether in the mother-baby relationship or affection for neighbours, our friends, or our work colleagues, as not demanding or expecting too much.[81] Lewis concludes that affection only produces happiness if there is a sense of give and take and an acceptation of common decency.

Lewis defines friendship/companionship as his second type of love, which may develop into erotic love and marriage because marrying our best friend is becoming more common in the western world in the 21st century.[82] Indeed, Lewis argues that having friends is extremely important to the survival of each individual in modern society. Jesus's disciples were called by him personally to be his friends,

---

79. C. S. Lewis. *The Four Loves*. William Collins, London, UK, 1960.
80. C. S. Lewis. *The Four Loves*. Chapter 3: "Affection."
81. Ibid.
82. C. S. Lewis. *The Four Loves*. Chapter 4: "Friendship."

even though one later betrayed him. True friends will be there for us when we are in crisis and require support. Friends and companions often have a lot in common, e.g., it could be a love of a sport in which they have similar experiences or thoughts on the sports team they support. It may be that they share other common interests, such as having children of the same age, or love for the arts; the list of common interests that could bring people together as companions/friends is exhaustive.

Lewis's third kind of love is eros, as described above, the act of falling in love with a partner including the sexual aspects of love.[83] Eros can include spiritual and carnal aspects of love and may focus on the love of a partner. Within eros, there is an element of us loving our partners as we love ourselves, and this can be referred back to the Biblical concept of a marriage where husbands are called to love their wives as they love themselves, but also both marriage partners are called to respect each other (Ephesians 5:22-23). Within eros, we should find that we love our partners deeply because love will cover over a multitude of sins (1 Peter 4:8).

It is sad that in our 21st-century societies, divorce rates remain high with the UK Office for National Statistics placing divorce rates in England and Wales over the past 50 years at 33.3%.[84] Of the couples who married 50 years ago in 1967, only 31.9% of their marriages had ended in divorce by 2017. In contrast, 43.6% of those marrying in 1987 had divorced by 2017, and 20.1% of

---

83. C. S. Lewis. *The Four Loves*. Chapter 5: "Eros."
84. https://www.nimblefins.co.uk/divorce-statistics-uk

couples married in 2007 had divorced within the first ten years by 2017. There are a number of reasons cited for divorce in the UK. The major cause for divorce in the UK varies depending on the gender of the spouse petitioning for divorce when considering opposite-sex couples. For men, the most widespread reason is a separation of over two years. For women, the most cited reason for wanting a divorce is the unreasonable behaviour of the spouse. However, these are not the only reasons for UK divorce proceedings. The other major reasons why UK couples divorce include the lack of preparation for married life, excessive arguing, infidelity, and the lack of equality within the marriage.[85]

Lewis's fourth type of love is termed charity which may be defined as the gift of love, or, as Lewis describes it, gift-love, meaning a love that gives, such as the mother feeding her baby.[86] Charity, as I understand it, provides a love that demands nothing in return. This kind of love comes through the grace of the giver. Lewis also states that God instils in each of us the need for love (need-love) from God and from one another. Lewis concludes that we are made for God and our supernatural love for God is what makes us and drives us forward.[87]

What is missing from our definition of love is how the Bible defines love. Love is patient, and patience is something that is in decline in our modern societies. Love is kind, not envious, boastful, proud, rude or selfish; it does

---

85. https://datingroo.co.uk/dating-after-divorce/divorce-rate/
86. C. S. Lewis. *The Four Loves*. Chapter 6: "Charity."
87. Ibid.

not keep a record of wrongs, it hates evil and rejoices in the truth. Love always perseveres, always hopes and is trusting; love provides protection, and most importantly for our society, love is not easily angered (1 Corinthians 13:4-7).

I have placed anger last because it is clear that our society has an increasing problem with anger. Statistics from mindyouranger.com show that General Practitioners have very few options available to help patients who come to them with anger issues.[88] They also report that 12% of people in the United Kingdom have difficulty in controlling their temper, with 28% admitting they are concerned with how angry they get and 20% of people admitting to ending a friendship or relationship with someone because they were afraid of how the person behaved when they were angry. *The Sunday Times* newspaper, on July 16, 2006, reported that 45% of people have lost their temper at work, with 64% of Britons admitting to experiencing office rage.[89] Other anger statistics revealed that 33% of people were not on speaking terms with their neighbours, more than 80% of drivers have been involved in road rage incidents and 25% of drivers admitted committing road rage. 71% of internet users admitted to net rage when their online searches didn't reveal the results they were looking for and 50% admitted hitting their computers as a result of bad search results. Also, 57% of people admitted losing their temper over the phone in the previous year. Overall, 64% of people agreed that in general, people are getting

---

88. https://www.mindyouranger.com/anger/anger-statistics/
89. Ibid.

angrier.[90] Jesus predicted that in the last days, because of the multiplication of wickedness, the love of most people will grow cold (Matthew 24:12), and this is linked with the intolerance we are seeing in our society. There is a deep requirement for more love, less judgement and intolerance and more patience.

This brings us full circle to the question, what is our understanding of the term 'God is love'? (1 John 4:8 and 4:16).

God is love

In the love of God, we should see each of the aspects of love described in the Bible's description of love found in 1 Corinthians 13: 4-7. Firstly, we should know and understand that love comes from God (1 John 4:7) and we cannot show genuine love without knowing God. We are able to love because God first loved us; our love is a response to God's love (1 John 4:19). The type of love we have here is agape love, a sacrificial love that drives God to love unconditionally, and being one in spirit and purpose with God and with our brethren/colleagues/partners (Philippians 2:2). God's love is practical and not theoretical, and is shown through him sending his son into the world to die for our sins so that we can be reconciled with God (1 John 4:9-10). God so loved the world that he sent his one and only son into the world to atone for our sins and transgressions, and anyone who believed in Jesus

---

90. Ibid.

as Lord and Saviour would have eternal life (John 3:16). Entrance into God's family is free, but membership costs us everything we have. We need to decide what we are seeking in this world, as the world is not our final resting place, and everything will pass away from the world.[91] Our home is in heaven.

God's love shown in patience and kindness

God's love is shown towards us in the patience he shows each one of us. A thousand earthly years is like a single day to God, and he patiently waits for us to repent and come to him (2 Peter 3:8-9). This can be illustrated by God waiting 400 years for the Amorites to repent before bringing his judgement upon them (Genesis 15:13-16). God waited patiently for Noah to complete building the ark before sending judgement on a wicked world (1 Peter 3:20). God would like us to become a people with patience in our dealings with others (Romans 15:5). How much better would the world be if all Christians were able to control their anger, and show patience towards others, regardless of how annoying those people are?

God declares himself to be compassionate, gracious, slow to lose his temper, full of love and faithfulness towards his people, maintaining his love towards his people, and forgiving the sins and wickedness of his peo-

---

91. Thomas A. Kempis. *The Imitation of Christ. Part 2.* Chapter 1: "On the inner life," pp. 53-55. Penguin Classics, Penguin Books, London, UK, 2013.

ple (Exodus 34:5-8). In showing his compassionate love for us, he hurls our iniquities into the depth of the sea (Micah 7:18). God's kindness toward us leads us toward repenting of our sins and accepting his love toward us (Romans 2:4). It is through God's gift of love and grace, which is expressed toward us through the sacrifice of Jesus on the cross, that we have been saved and brought into God's family (Ephesians 2:7). God showed his patience toward Israel for many years before he brought down his judgement on the Nation (Nehemiah 9:30). However, God's patience does not last forever; there will be a time when God will say time is up, my judgement is upon you. God is gracious, compassionate, isn't easily angered and is full of love and faithfulness toward his people (Exodus 34:5-8). Through Jesus, God provides peace and grace in the present evil age and has rescued us from the guilt and consequences of the present evil age (Galatians 1:4). God has raised us up to be seated with Christ on a heavenly throne that he may show us the riches of his love and grace and his eternal kindness for those who love him (Ephesians 2:6-9).

Love keeps no record of wrongs and this is true for God in so much that he has forgiven our sins and iniquities and no longer remembers our wickedness (Isaiah 43:25; Hebrews 8:12 and 10:17). So, we can conclude with confidence that God's love for us is immense.

Reconciling God's love with a wicked world

One of the main questions about the belief in God in the Western World today is why does God allow suffering for good people? We can understand when bad things happen to bad people; our response is usually that they deserve it. However, we struggle with bad things happening to people who we perceive as being good people. The same question perplexed some of the authors in the Old Testament. Habakkuk was puzzled by God's inactivity among the wrongs and violence of his day (Habakkuk 1:2-4). Why does God allow war? Why are we seeing a war in Ukraine at the moment and why are innocent people being so mercilessly murdered by the invading forces? What on earth is God going to do about it? How can a loving, caring God allow such atrocities? The Bible asserts that God is sovereign over all the earth, that God started history and that he is controlling history and he will end history at the proper designated time.[92] In times of stress and difficulties, men and women turn instinctively to God, so difficulties occur to draw us closer to God.[93] Perhaps in times of stress and challenges, we are more aware of the presence of God than when there are positive circumstances in our lives. Indeed, we are haunted by the need to make sense of things, more so during times of stress than when all things are relatively rosy in our

---

92. Martyn Lloyd-Jones. *From Fear to Faith: Rejoicing in the Lord in Turbulent Times.* Chapter 1: "The strangeness of God's ways," pp. 13-22. Inter Varsity Press, Nottingham, UK, 1997.

93. Martyn Lloyd-Jones. *Why Does God Allow War?* Chapter 1: "Man in the presence of God," pp. 15-16. Crossway Books, Illinois, USA, 2003.

lives.[94] We have already alluded to God waiting 400 years for the Amorites to repent before bringing his judgement upon them (Genesis 15:13-16). However, during this time, God's chosen people Israel were slaves in Egypt and went through considerable hardship and despair. God is so full of love that he does not want anyone to perish but all men and women to come to eternal life (2 Peter 3:9). Therefore, God's bigger picture is to bring us to repentance and a greater dependence on him, which ultimately will bring us to eternal life and heavenly paradise. In this respect, we have been created for fellowship with God and only God can satisfy our deepest longings.[95]

A second reason why there is so much suffering in this present world is that it is a fallen world full of sin and rebellion. This present earth is under the control of Satan (1 John 5:19). For those who believe in Christ as their Lord and Saviour, this earth is not our final destination, and we are not of this world, therefore, those of the world hate Christians because we are not like them and do not conform to their standards (John 15:19). Failure to grasp that we are "other-worldly" accounts for much of the unhappiness in the lives of Christian people, and for our disappointment with God when bad things come our way.[96]

---

94. Alister McGrath. *Glimpsing the Face of God*. Chapter 5: "The great narrative of our destiny," p. 46. Lion Books, Oxford, UK, 2002.
95. Ibid., p. 51.
96. Martyn Lloyd-Jones. *Why Does God Allow War?* Chapter 5: "The final answer to all our questions," pp. 112-116. Crossway Books, Illinois, USA, 2003.

What is man?

God has shown his great love for us by saving us from eternal damnation for our sins. He has shown his great compassion for us in meeting us where we stand, and Jesus's compassion can be seen in the feeding of the hungry, in the raising of Lazarus from the dead, and in the many healings and miracles he performed when he was on the earth. Jesus could only do what he saw his father in heaven doing, so the miracles were done at the father's will (John 5:19). We come to the question that is posed in Psalm 8:4 "What is man that he is constantly part of your thinking, or the son of man that you care for him?" The answer to this question is central to everything, or, to put it another way, the answer to life, the universe and everything in it. Christian belief and Biblical teaching hold that a loving God created the universe and that life on earth is not a consequence of a cosmic accident.[97] Despite the massive advances in science over the last 100 years or so, scientists are unable to exclude the possibility that the universe came into being through an act of God.[98] The answer to why God considers men and women lies in the fact that we were created in the image of God (Genesis 1:26-27). It is this fact that sets us apart from all the animals and plants that cohabit the planet with us. Before we became Christians, we were a slave to our self-expressions and lusts, our sexual impulses, greed, selfishness, ambition, lawless acts, hatred, anger and all kinds of rebellions (Galatians 5:19-22). Through the

---

97. Alister McGrath, ibid., pp. 46-51.
98. Stephen Hawking, ibid.

Holy Spirit, we are slowly being transformed into our original purpose to conform to the likeness or image of Christ. It is for this purpose that God has not given up on men or women and has poured out his great love upon us.

What should our response be to God's great love toward us? We love God because he first loved us (1 John 4:10). Therefore, we must shape our desires to come into line with those laid down by God.[99] We must have a real desire for holiness and to thirst and hunger after righteousness (Matthew 5:6).[100] If our citizenship is in heaven then we should glorify or esteem God at every level of our lives.[101] Our aim should be to glorify God in every aspect of our daily lives and live with our hearts always towards heaven.[102] Many of our problems will shrink when we learn to magnify and glorify God and value God above the things that are hindering us and to truly value the things and love of God.[103]

---

99. Thomas A. Kempis. *The Imitation of Christ. Part 4.* Chapter 11: "The desires of the heart," p. 140. Penguin Classics, Penguin Books, London, UK, 2013.
100. Thomas A. Kempis. *The Imitation of Christ. Part 3.* Chapter 15: "How true devotion is gained," p. 114. Penguin Classics, Penguin Books, London, UK, 2013.
101. William Law. *A Serious Call to a Devout and Holy Life.* Chapter 4: "Whatever state we are in," pp. 28-29. Hodder & Stoughton, London, 1987.
102. Ibid., pp. 34-37.
103. Andrew Wommack. *Discover the Keys to Staying full of God.* Chapter 4 and 5: "What do you value?" and "Set joy before you," pp. 25-41. Andrew Wommack Ministries-Europe, Walsall, England, 2019.

Prayer

Dearest Heavenly Father, we thank you for your great love for us that while we were still steeped in our sins and iniquities, Christ died for us. We are grateful that you reached out to us with your great love and are thankful that we could enter into your family by calling upon the name of Jesus as our Lord and Saviour. We are thankful that you have shared everything in heaven and on earth with us and we wish to respond to you by giving you all our love in return. I lift up before you right now all my sins and iniquities and ask your forgiveness for often going my own way without any consideration for you. We commit ourselves totally to your mercy and goodness and place ourselves completely in your hands.[104] In Jesus's name we pray. Amen

---

104. Thomas A. Kempis. *The Imitation of Christ. Part 3*. Chapter 9: "We should offer ourselves totally," p. 100.

8.

The peace of God

The state of the world

When we consider peace, two things come to mind; firstly, that we can think of peace in terms of deliverance from war, and secondly, we can remember such things as the celebrations that occurred at the end of the Second World War, with the victory in Europe (VE) celebrations as Nazi Germany surrendered. The outcome of this war was seen as the triumph of good over evil. We can consider the wars that are occurring around the world, such as the war in Ukraine occurring in 2022 and the struggles of the Ukrainian people to win the war with Russia and return to peace. When we consider the world, it is clear that the world is not the way it was meant to be.[105] Milton referred to the world as paradise lost and sums up our present condition as:

---

105. Alister McGrath. *Glimpsing the Face of God.* Chapter 9: "The great anomaly," p. 91. Lion Books, Oxford, UK, 2002.

Where then there is no good
For which to strive, no strife can grow up there
From faction; for none sure will claim in hell…
Whether of open war or covert guile,
We now debate who can advise…
My sentence is for open war of wiles.[106]

The most important consideration is that Jesus warned us that in the end times of this present age, there would be wars and rumours of wars (Matthew 24:6), so we shouldn't be surprised or unduly worried when these things occur. It is important to note that wars occur as a consequence of the sins of individual leaders, and because of the sins of the countries that these leaders represent.[107] War reveals the sinfulness of human nature, how despicably low men can stoop in their sinful nature, and the despicable depths of sin as mankind attempts to justify their actions.[108] However, the present world will end and pass away, and be replaced by a world without pain and suffering, a paradise regained (Revelation 21:1).[109]

The second approach to considering peace is in terms of our relationship with God. The Bible has a lot to say about the peace of God, and, from the start, that the wicked have no peace (Isaiah 48:22). We can see that the present world lies in the hands of Satan, and we should not

---

106. John Milton. *Paradise Lost,* Book II: "The argument," p. 25, stanzas 30-50. Penguin Books, London, England, 2003.
107. Martyn Lloyd-Jones. *Why Does God Allow War?* Chapter 4: "Why does God allow war?," pp. 95-98. Crossway Books, Illinois, USA, 2003.
108. Ibid., pp. 94-96.
109. Alister McGrath, ibid., pp. 91-96.

be surprised that it is a world with much wickedness, that as we move nearer to the end of this present age, evil will abound more and more (1 John 5:19). God has no pleasure in the death of the wicked but hopes that they may turn from their wickedness and be saved (Ezekiel 33:11). God will bring to a day of judgement the righteous and the wicked, and we are told that before God's great throne in the place of judgement, wickedness was there (Ecclesiastes 3:16-17). The wicked will not go unpunished; the wicked are valueless, and will be removed from the land and from God's presence (Proverbs 2:22; 10:20; 11:21). The wicked will perish and the righteous will have eternal life (Psalm 1:5; Ezekiel 3:18). Also, the righteous are called not to worry about evil men for the Lord has promised that ultimately, they will not prosper but instead will wither and die away (Psalm 37:1-2). However, God takes no pleasure in the death of the wicked (Ezekiel 18:23).

Another consideration that is popular in the 21st century, is that if God is a God of love, he should not allow the righteous to suffer as they often do in this fallen world, and a loving God would not allow wars and other catastrophes to exist and flourish in the world.[110] However, God's ways are not our ways and much of what God is doing in this world today is a mystery to us. God's ways are high above what we can imagine, but the Bible promises that God's will be done on earth as it is in heaven (Isaiah 55:8-9). Following the fall of man, evil was introduced into the world because of the disobedience of Adam and Eve in the gar-

---

110. Martyn Lloyd-Jones. *Why Does God Allow War?* Chapter 3: "The mysteries of God's ways," p. 65. Crossway Books, Illinois, USA, 2003.

den of Eden. Evil can be defined as wrongdoing, doing things that are opposed or forbidden by God. Wickedness can be defined as deliberately doing what God has forbidden or going against God's laws, such as those laid out in the 10 commandments (Deuteronomy 5:6-21). At this point, God had two choices; firstly, to destroy mankind and start again, or secondly, to allow things to develop in the world and to bring salvation to the lost through Jesus Christ our Lord. Right from the start of fallen mankind, God chose the second option (Genesis 3:14-15). It didn't take long before murder entered the world (Genesis 4:8). Since the time of Cain and Abel, there have been multiple troubles and strife within the world, but take heart because Jesus has overcome the difficulties that occur in the world (John 16:33). Julian of Norwich described sin as a scourge that destroys men and women to the degree that they can only sink down into hell.[111]

Peace of God

When we consider our individual lives, then it is good to be at peace in ourselves and with God, and we can rest assured that Jesus gives his peace to his followers (John 14:27). On the eve of his death, Jesus gave his peace to us and what a wonderful peace it is to have. Of all the gifts he could have left behind, being at peace with ourselves and at peace with God is the most important factor in an evil world. It

---

111. Julian of Norwich. *Revelations of Divine Love*. Chapter 17, p. 26. Translated by Elizabeth Spearing. Penguin Classics, UK, 1998.

is reassuring to know that Jesus is the Lord of peace and that he has given us his peace at all times and in every circumstance that we face each day (2 Thessalonians 3:16). We have been called to peace, and are encouraged to allow the peace of God to dwell in our hearts at all times, and in all situations we face in life (Colossians 3:15). One of the fruits of the Holy Spirit is the fruit of peace (Galatians 5:22). It is reassuring to know that even if the mountains and hills fall away and are destroyed, God's covenant of peace will remain (Isaiah 54:10). Our faith in Jesus of Nazareth as our Lord and Saviour is the foundation of our peace with God (Romans 5:1).

As long as our minds are focused upon Jesus, then God will keep us in perfect peace (Isaiah 26:3). We should always keep before us the fact that all that we accomplish in this world is accomplished through Christ (Isaiah 26:12). In this respect, we should rest assured that nothing happens by accident or luck; everything occurs through the will and grace of God.[112]

Practicality of peace with God

We must realise that peace with God can only be achieved through the acceptance of our Lord Jesus Christ as our Lord and Saviour. This leads to repentance, which is relinquishing our old sinful life with worldly desires and setting out in a new direction with God, where God's commandments and precepts become our main desire. In other terms, we

---

112. Ibid., Chapter 8, p. 12.

move from the darkness into the light (1 John 1:5). We kill those things in our lives that are opposed to the will of God. We make God the centre of our goals and ambitions and leave behind everything that is opposed to God.

In the turmoil that is life, even when we are walking in God's plan for our lives, we may face opposition and obstacles, as the disciples did when Jesus sent them out ahead of him in the fishing boat at night (Matthew 14:22-36). At first, the boat was buffeted while Jesus stayed behind to pray, but in the midst of the storm, Jesus came, and he came in a miraculous way, walking on the water. Jesus was above the waves and was not hindered in any way by the storm. The second point from the account of Jesus walking on water is that if we are going to reach our goals, and fulfil God's purpose for our lives, we have to get out of the boat (Matthew 14:28). It is a fact of life that most of us prefer to stay in the comfort of the boat. Peter was the only disciple to get out of the boat, and while he kept his eyes on Jesus, he was able to overcome the storm and walk on water. The truth is that while we keep our eyes on Jesus and not on the storm, we will be operating in the realm of the supernatural. However, the moment we take our eyes away from Jesus and focus on the waves that are buffeting us, then we begin to sink. It is our faith in Jesus that sustains us through the storms of life and enables us to overcome the obstacles we face on our journey through life with God. Jesus rebuked Peter for his lack of faith and for doubting that he could overcome the waves. Without faith, it is impossible to please God (Hebrews 11:6). If we keep our eyes upon Jesus then our faith will not fail us regardless of the storms that surround us. Notice that as soon as Jesus entered the boat, the storm died down and stopped. The storms in life are often sent by God to test our faith because God wants our faith and belief in him to grow and become stronger. God tests our faith so that we may persevere, and through perseverance, we mature and grow in our faith, so that we lack nothing (James 1:3-4).

When we face the storms of life, we are called not to be anxious or worried about the outcome, but to pray and be thankful that God hears our prayers (Philippians 4:6). Pray first and rejoice with thankfulness and then the peace of God that surpasses and exceeds our understanding will keep our hearts and minds safe from turmoil (Philippians 4:7). Part of remaining at peace in our circumstances and remaining within the peace of God is to focus on good things and positive thoughts, to think about things that excel and are worthy of our thanksgiving and praise (Philippians 4:9). In other words, take our minds off the problems and focus on Jesus.

Our role in the peace of God

Jesus left us his peace and it is in our hands to receive that peace and not to let our hearts be overcome with troubles (John 14:27). To remain in the peace that Jesus gave us, we have to learn from him, and be imitators of Christ, and be gentle and humble of heart (Matthew 11:29). We shouldn't let our peace depend upon what other people think of us.[113] We are called to keep the unity of the Spirit, which is held together by the bond of peace (Ephesians 4:3). The biggest challenge for us today is to control our anger, to remain at peace, and not to fall out with those with whom we interact every day, whether they be family, neighbours, or work colleagues. We are called to live in peace (2 Corinthians 13:11). We can only achieve this if we keep our eyes fixed upon Jesus, and are not judgmental of other people, however annoying they may be. If our mind is governed by God's Spirit then we will remain at peace, no matter whatever life throws our way (Romans 8:6). If we trust God in all our circumstances, then our minds will be kept in perfect peace (Isaiah 26:3). The challenge is to keep our minds continually fixed upon God, and then we will find that peace is a blessing from God (Psalm 29:11). We are called to make every effort to live peacefully with those we come in contact with in our daily lives (Hebrews 12:14; Romans 12:18). We are to sow in peace in order to reap a harvest of righteousness before God (James 3:18), and to actively pursue the peace of God (1 Peter 3:11), knowing that the gospel of Christ brings peace (Ephesians 6:15). We can then go out with the joy of the Lord and be led forward in his peace (Isaiah 55:12). Jesus, through the Holy Spirit, reveals things to us that are about to come to fruition, so that we may have peace (John 16:33). Ultimately, God is a God of peace (1 Corinthians 14:33), and we have peace with God through our Lord Jesus Christ (Romans 5:1).

---

113. Thomas A. Kempis. *The Imitation of Christ. Part 4.* Chapter 28: "Against slanderous talk," p. 170.

Assurance of peace

On the eve of his death, knowing that the disciples were troubled by his imminent departure from them, Jesus told the disciples not to be worried, but rather to trust in God and to trust in him (John 14:1). Whatever, is happening in the world or in our lives, we can trust in God and in Jesus. We need to be assured of our peace and our place in heaven by looking to God and Jesus. The focus for all believers, in a world that will become darker and more evil, is to keep our eyes focused and fixed on God and Jesus. In this respect, Jesus has promised to be with us even to the end of the earth; he will never leave us or forsake us (Matthew 28:20). We have the assurance that whoever calls on Jesus's name will be saved and will be among the saved (Romans 10:13). When we are in distress, we can ask and seek God; we are assured we will find him, and he will open the door to us and restore our peace (Matthew 7:8; Matthew 21:22). We should give thanks to the Lord because he will deliver us from the evil one, and the redeemed of the Lord can thank him for all manner of deliverances (Psalm 107). Whether we are in a desert, hungry and thirsty, sitting in darkness and deepest gloom, prisoners in our own homes or environments, feel like we are chained up and unable to move, feel like we are near the gates of death, or at our wit's end, God will save us and deliver us.

If the worse things in life work together for the good of those who love the Lord (Romans 8:28), think that the best things will work for us who believe.[114] If God makes all things work for our good then we should be free to give him the glory.[115] We should always be thankful for what God is doing in our lives, no matter how dark the world seems to us. We can never be truly at peace until we have a right relationship with God, and the only person that can put us in a right relationship with God is Jesus Christ our Lord.[116]

---

114. Thomas Watson. *All Things for Good*. Chapter 3: "Why all things work for good to the godly," p. 63. Banner of Truth Trust, Edinburgh, UK. First published 1663, reprinted 2001

115. Ibid.

116. Martyn Lloyd-Jones. *Let Not Your Heart Be Troubled*. Chapter 3: "Believe also in me," p. 57. Crossway, Illinois, USA, 2009.

Prayer

Dear Heavenly Father, we thank you that you are always with us even to the end of the age, that you are with us in the good times and in the bad times of our lives, and we can always rely upon you to bless us and bring us through to the very end. We thank you, Jesus, that you have given us your peace that passes all understanding, and that we can rely upon you to guide us and lead us in every situation and every circumstance we find ourselves in. Dearest Lord, we know that all things work together for our good and that we are called to persevere and keep our eyes fixed on you at all times. Abba Father, thank you that you have promised that all who call upon the Lord Jesus will be saved and will, on that final day, be transported to be with Jesus and to be like him. Help us in this darkening world to always keep our eyes on our final destination which is to be in heaven with you. Thank you, God, in Jesus's name we pray, Amen.

9.

Chosen by God

THOSE WHO HAVE accepted Jesus as their Lord and Saviour are welcomed into God's family. The invitation to join God's family is given to all who receive Jesus of Nazareth as their Lord and Saviour (John 1:12). We are born again by the will of God and join his family. The Bible tells us that God chose us to be part of his family before he created the world (Ephesians 1:4). Before we were formed in our mother's womb, God knew us and set us apart to be a member of his family (Jeremiah 1:4-5). It is not by chance that we have accepted Jesus as our Lord and Saviour. God has adopted us as his sons and daughters to be part of his family for eternity, and it was God's pleasure to be chosen by him to be destined to be with him for eternity. There is nothing special that would make us stand out from others that inspired God to choose us but he did. He made his decision long before we came into the world, so nothing was left to chance. We have the great privilege to be chosen by the Living God, the Almighty God, who is from everlasting to everlasting, to be part of his family forever. That is the good news of the gospel. We are redeemed from death and darkness to the light that is God and to eternal life.

God's plan

From the very beginning, God has made us part of his eternal plan, so that we may bring glory to his holy name among the people of the earth. God chose us out of all the people on the face of the earth to be his treasured possessions (Deuteronomy 7:6). It is good to know that we are precious and treasured in God's sight and that he greatly delights in who we are. God's choice in us is unconditional, and he never bases his choice on the way that men think, and God's choice of who he saves is not based on any attribute of man or woman.[117] The good news gets better and better, in so much as all believers have been marked in him with the seal of the Holy Spirit (Ephesians 1:13). It is God's plan to give a singleness of heart so that we will fear him for our own good and for the good of our children (Jeremiah 32:38-39). God rejoices in doing good for each one of us and in leading us deeper into a life of holiness before him and with him (Jeremiah 32:40-41). God aims to inspire us to never turn away from him, but always to be focused on our goal, which is that we are passing through the earth on our journey to eternal life with God.

---

117. Edwin H. Palmer. *The Five Points of Calvinism*. Chapter 2: "Unconditional election," p. 31. Baker Books, Grand Rapids, MI, USA, 1972.

Jesus chose us out of the world, to be separate from the world (John 15:19). We have grace and peace from God because of Christ's redemptive sacrifice in dying for our sins on the cross in order to rescue us from the darkness of this present evil world (Galatians 1:1-3). God chose us out of the world because we are weak, because we are foolish, and because we were despised (1 Corinthians 1:27-29). The good news is that we are a chosen people, part of a holy nation, called out of the darkness of this evil world into his glorious light, so that we may declare the praises of our God (1 Peter 2:9). Jesus promises us that all who come to him will be accepted and that he is our bread of life; we will never go hungry or thirsty (John 6:35-37). Nobody can come to Jesus unless the Father has sanctioned it, and everyone who has been predestined to be with God will be resurrected on the last day when Jesus comes again (John 6:44). Jesus tells us that we did not choose him but he chose us, so that we may go out and further the Kingdom of Heaven by bearing fruit (John 15:16). Jesus also knows his sheep and as Christians, we are the sheep who know the Lord (John 10:14). What is of interest is that when Paul and Barnabas preached to the Gentiles, we are told that all who had been chosen by God to eternal life believed the message and were saved (Acts 13:48). It is exciting to know that God was able to motivate and move those who he had chosen to a place where they could hear the gospel and be saved. It is important to know that the elect did not make a decision before hearing the gospel message, and therefore, this is why it is so important to preach the word of God to the lost. We should never forget that faith in Jesus comes from hearing the gospel, and the gospel is preached through the word of Jesus (Romans 10:17). It is important to consider that the church in the United Kingdom is failing in its outreach as church numbers have dropped in most denominations by between 20% and 81% in the years from 1980 to 2015.[118] The only church growth according to the statistics is in the Pentecostal and New church denominations. Those who are saved are saved through the sanctifying work of the Holy Spirit and through their faith and belief in the word of God (2 Thessalonians 2:13).

God has called us by name and we will not be overcome by the deluge of life or the fires and crises that may come our way in this evil world (Isaiah 43:1-3). We are precious, honoured and greatly loved by God (Isaiah 43:4). We can call upon God when we are in trouble and he has promised to deliver us (Psalm 50:15).

Our response to destiny

We are warned not to love the things of the world, or to crave and lust after the things of the world (John 1:15-17). The things we are warned to avoid include lusting with our eyes. We have been warned not to lust after women and, by inclination, for women not to lust after men (Matthew 5:28), because we have sinned in our hearts.

---

118. http://www.brin.ac.uk/figures/church-attendance-in-britain-1980-2015

However, lust goes further than that, in as much that we can lust after clothes or possessions or a different life. We are also warned not to lust after riches or the things that the world prides above others, such as ambition in our careers, etc.

We were predestined to be transformed into the likeness of Jesus (Romans 8:29). God chooses who he has compassion on and he chooses who to show mercy to (Romans 9:15). It is a privileged position that believers find themselves in and we must never take our position in Christ for granted. We are called not to conform with the world standards but to be transformed or metamorphosed or renovated through the renewing of our minds (Romans 12:2). Renewing our minds is something that we must actively carry out by focusing upon the truth, whatever is noble, pure, lovely, praiseworthy and the like (Philippians 4:6-9). We are instructed to clothe ourselves with compassion, gentleness, patience, humility and kindness (Colossians 3:12). Compassion is something that is in short supply in today's society. Few of us have real empathy for the distress of other people, but compassion is an important attribute for all Christians to acquire. To be gentle and kind toward the people we come into contact with should be an attribute of every believer. To focus on things that are praiseworthy, pure and lovely is a challenge in today's world when there is so much hurt and pain transported into our living rooms through the news, current affairs programmes, the media in general, advertising and the like.

What we become

When we accept Christ as our Lord and Saviour, we become new creations. Our old life in darkness has died, and we are born again (2 Corinthians 5:17). We cannot see the Kingdom of God without being born again in the Holy Spirit (John 3:3-6). We can do nothing without it being provided for us by God (John 3:27). God prepared our good works in advance of us; therefore, it is up to us to carry out these good works to the glory of God (Ephesians 2:10).

It is noteworthy to reflect on the fact that when Jesus declared that he was the bread of life, and that anyone who eats the bread of life and drinks of his blood will be saved and have eternal life (John 6:48-58), many disciples found it difficult to accept. Certainly, we too will find some of the things that Jesus asks of us in this life to be difficult, but we are entrusted by God to carry them out and continue with Jesus to the end. The testing of our faith produces perseverance and patience, and if we endure the trials and tribulations of life, we will receive the crown of life from Jesus (James 1:2-4 and 12).

There is no doubt that dark times are coming upon the earth when evil will abound, and there will be many trials for Christians before the coming of the Lord. Jesus has promised that those who overcome will be able to eat from the tree of life which is in the middle of the paradise of God (Revelation 2:7); when under persecution, those who persevere are promised safety from the second death (Revelation 2:10); those who keep God's works until the end will be given the power to rule over nations (Revelation 2:26); if our faith is failing us and we begin to grow cold and give up, Jesus calls us to repent and return to him, and if we are able to do that then we will be given the garments and righteousness and not be removed from God's Book of Life (Revelation 3:5); for those of us who have little strength, Jesus has promised an open door that cannot be shut, and we will be made pillars in the temple of God and will be given a new name (Revelation 3:12). If we remain hot for God and turned on to do his work regardless of the cost then Jesus has promised that we may sit down on his throne with him (Revelation 3:21). Jesus has warned us that it is difficult for a rich man to enter the Kingdom of God, because he is likely to put his wealth before the work of God (Matthew 19:23). However, all things are possible with God and nothing is too difficult for him, therefore, we should always keep our eyes fixed upon the Lord and not on the torrent of circumstances that surround us (Matthew 19:26).

Stay strong even until the end, and know that no eye has seen, nor have they heard, nor has anyone conceived what God has in store for those who love him, but God reveals such things to those who love him by his Spirit (1 Corinthians 2:9-10). As we have stated earlier, Jesus has gone ahead of us to prepare a place for each one of us in his Father's mansion in paradise (John 14:2).

Prayer

Dear Heavenly Father, thank you that out of all the world, you chose us to be your loyal and faithful servants. We are so grateful that no eye has seen, no mind has imagined what you have prepared for those who love you and are called according to your purposes. Help us, dear Lord, to always be faithful to you regardless of our circumstances, and enable us to keep our eyes fixed on the prize of one day being in paradise with you. Lord, it is reassuring to know that you chose us before the foundation of the world and that you are with us every step of our lives. Thank you, Lord, that you have gone ahead of us to prepare a place for us in your Father's mansion. Thank you, Lord, for always being by our sides. In Jesus's name we pray. Amen.

10.

The God who heals

The need for healing

We live in a fallen world where we toil for a living in a ground that is cursed beneath our feet, and we were formed from dust and will return at death to the dust (Genesis 3:19). Jesus told us that during the end times, there would be famines, pestilences and earthquakes (Matthew 24:7-8). So, it should not be a surprise when pestilences such as the plague, malaria, tuberculosis, influenza, Ebola, methicillin-resistant *Staphylococcus aureus*, most commonly called MRSA, AIDS, Covid-19 and, most recently, Monkeypox break out on mankind. Above I have listed infectious diseases, but some diseases that frighten us the most are not infectious, such as cancer, stroke and heart disease to name a few. Then we have the four horsemen of the apocalypse where the fourth horseman was given the power to kill a quarter of the earth by sword, famine and plague (Revelation 6:7-8). Our failings to keep God's commandments also bring the danger of disease being placed upon God's servants (Exodus 15:26; Deuteronomy 7:15; Leviticus 26:16). We also see that Jesus warned the man that healed at the pool of Siloam not to sin again or something worse may come upon him (John 5:14). Does that mean that all the pestilences and diseases that we see in the world are because of God's judgement? The answer is a strong no. Rather, there are many reasons for disease to be in the world, including to focus our attention on Jesus; we are called to repent not because of pestilences and plagues but because of Jesus himself.[119] As Tom Wright points out, plagues may indeed be messengers from God,[120] that the time to repent and return to him is short, and the clock is ticking toward the end of the age.

Not all disease occurs because God is judging us for our sins, even though many Christians, and indeed, Jesus's own disciples made the assumption that disease is God's judgement. As we see with the healing of the blind man, where neither the sin of the blind man nor his parents was responsible for his condition, but rather he was born blind to bring glory to God (John 9:1-7). Also, some afflictions may occur to prove our faith, as with Job (Job 2:7). Our faith can make us well as with the woman who had been bleeding for 12 years (Matthew 9:20-22), and the blind men (Matthew 9:27-31). Healing can take place as a testimony to the world, as with the healing of the mute demon-possessed man (Matthew 9:32-33).

---

119. Tom Wright. *God and the Pandemic: A Christian Reflection on the Coronavirus and Its Aftermath*, p. 37. SPCK, London, UK, 2020.
120. Ibid., p. 63.

Illness may fall upon us to prevent us from becoming conceited, and to keep us focused upon God, the author and perfector of our faith (2 Corinthians 12:7-10).

It is important at this point to notice that the whole of creation is groaning because of the fall of man (Romans 8:22-27), and it is not surprising that we are close to passing the point of no return in global warming, which, in itself, leads to natural disasters such as an increase in the frequency of earthquakes, volcanoes, tsunamis and the like.

Healing from death

When we consider being healed by God, then we should know that being reconciled to God through the blood of Jesus, who died on the cross for our iniquities, is the greatest healing of all. The wages of sin are death for all who are in the kingdom of darkness and separated from the love of God, but the free gift of God is eternal life for all those who accept Jesus as their Lord and Saviour (Romans 6:23). We have passed over from death to eternal life, and death no longer holds any fear. Death no longer holds a sting but is consumed in the resurrection of the body to eternity (1 Corinthians 15:54-55). We will be raised from the dead to eternal life with an imperishable spiritual body, and we will bear the image of Christ and be like him (1 Corinthians 15:40-55). All men and women will experience the first death, which is the decay and death of our earthly bodies, but then we will be blessed with a spiritual body.

When Jesus died on the cross, the barrier between God and men was broken as symbolised by the tearing of the curtain in the Temple in Jerusalem (Matthew 27:51). Then the tombs in the cemeteries throughout Jerusalem were opened and the bodies of the holy believers in Christ were raised to life (Matthew 27:52). These holy people who were raised from the dead went throughout Jerusalem appearing to people (Matthew 27:53). We can imagine the scene throughout Jerusalem when these holy people were going through the city speaking to people. Imagine the shock of their relatives when confronted by these people raised from the dead—great funeral by the way and we loved the eulogy, however, we are just off to heaven with Jesus the Messiah, but it's been great talking with you.

After the death of Jesus on the cross, it was natural for Jesus's followers to go to his tomb to find him, but the stone was rolled away and Jesus was not there. He had already risen from the dead (Mark 16:1-8; John 20:1-9). When Jesus was raised from the dead and before he ascended into heaven, we are told that he appeared to many people in a variety of circumstances. Firstly, Jesus appeared to two of the disciples on the road to Emmaus (Luke 24:13-32). Even after his death, Jesus had to explain to the disciples why he had to die but notice this; as soon as the disciples recognised Jesus, he disappeared from their sight. The important point is that when we receive our spiritual bodies, we will no longer be constrained by the laws of science. After he was resurrected, Jesus appeared to Mary Magdalene (John 20:10-18). When Jesus appeared to the disciples, he brought his peace with him (Luke 24:36; John 20:19). He made a second visitation to the disciples to placate Thomas's doubt about the resurrection (John 20:24-29). Jesus had a special visitation with Peter to reinstate him after he had denied Jesus (John 21:15-22). We are told that before Jesus ascended into heaven, he appeared to over 500 people who are all witnesses to his resurrection (1 Corinthians 15:6). The greatest healing that Jesus brings to men and women is the healing over death.

Healing on the earth

Jesus took upon himself our ailments, diseases, illnesses, maladies and sicknesses (Isaiah 53:4), and through the wounds afflicted upon him, we are healed (Isaiah 53:5). It is worth noting that in 2021, 30% of people living in the UK suffered from at least one mental health disorder. This compared with 17% in Denmark, 22% in Spain, 24% in Italy, 25% in Germany, and 27% in France and Sweden.[121] In part due to the Covid-19 pandemic, mental health issues are becoming more pronounced among us and are an increasing global problem in the 21st century. Covid-19 has been reported as having a negative impact on mental health in between 44% of people living in Denmark and 65% of people living in the UK.[122] Worldwide, 792 million (10.7% of the world's popula-

---

121. https://www.statista.com/statistics/1196047/mental-health-illness-prevalence-in-europe-by-country/
122. https://www.statista.com/statistics/1196014/impact-of-covid-19-on-mental-health-in-europe/

tion) people were reported as suffering from at least one mental health disorder affecting 9.3% of men and 11.9% of women.[123] Overall, 12.8% of young people between the ages of 5-19 years meet the criteria for a mental health disorder.[124] Furthermore, suicide is the leading cause of death in the 5-19-year-old age group in the UK, and over the past 5 years, has increased by 23% in the same age group in the USA.[125]

Jesus healed many of their various diseases and maladies, which no doubt would include mental health issues (Mark 1:29-33). However, among those with mental health issues, anxiety and depression are the key symptoms, and we can rely upon Jesus to help us with these symptoms: cast all our anxieties upon him, which will be replaced with his peace (Philippians 4:6). Jesus cares about our anxieties and troubles (1 Peter 5:7). God offers hope and a future for all who trust him, and his love for us, regardless of our circumstances, underlines a way to a better future (Jeremiah 29:7).

While on earth, Jesus healed a paralytic (Mark 2:1-13), healed a demon-possessed man (Mark 5:1-21), raised Jairus's daughter from the dead, and healed a woman who had been subject to bleeding for 12 years (Mark 5:22-43). He went through towns and villages in Israel healing every kind of disease (Matthew 9:35): He healed the centurion's servant (Luke 7:1-10); He had compassion on the wid-

123. https://ourworldindata.org/mental-health
124. https://mhfaengland.org/mhfa-centre/research-and-evaluation/mental-health-statistics/
125. https://www.unilad.co.uk/featured/suicide-kills-young-people-cause-death/

ow's son and raised him from the dead (Luke 7:11-16); He raised Lazarus from the dead (John 11:38-44).

It is noteworthy to point out that Jesus also healed those who were socially excluded from society. Leprosy in Jesus's day held the same fear and social stigma that bubonic plague held for those living in the 14th to 16th centuries, smallpox held in the 18th and 19th centuries and AIDS held in the latter part of the 20th century. Jesus not only healed people with leprosy but he crossed the Jewish convention of the day by reaching out and touching someone who was considered by society as being unclean and an outcast (Matthew 8:1-4). Jesus had already indicated that the law set out by Moses would not pass away until heaven and earth passed away (Matthew 5:17), and in regards to the leper, Jesus sent him to the priest to fulfil the requirements of the law as described in Leviticus 14:1-32. The leper would have to be cleared by a priest and verified that he had been healed before being allowed back into society.

Promises of healing

There are many promises in the Bible regarding the healing of those who believe and call upon the name of the Lord. The prayers of the righteous are powerful and there is a need to confess our sins in order that we may be healed (James 5:16). If we call for God's help, he will heal us (Psalm 30:2): God will sustain us on our sick beds and restore us from our illness (Psalm 41:3): God will save us from the deadly pestilence and disease (Psalm 91:3): There is no need to fear plagues and pestilences because it will not come near us (Psalm 91:6-8): God heals all our diseases (Psalm 103:2): God heals us and delivers us from our distress (Psalm 107:20): If God heals us, we will be healed (Jeremiah 17:14): God will restore us to health (Jeremiah 30:17): God will heal us and bind up our wounds when we return to him (Hosea 6:1).

Greater things shall we accomplish

Jesus promised that those who have faith in him will be able to do the things that he had done during his earthly ministry and would be able to do even greater things once Jesus had returned to heaven (John 14:12). The Holy Spirit was sent for the good of mankind and among the gifts that we receive from the Holy Spirit is the gift of healing (1 Corinthians 12:9). In the church, God has appointed those with the gift of healing (1 Corinthians 12:28). The ministry of healing in the early church was carried out by the elders in the church (James 5:14) but was not limited to the elders alone. At the Temple in Jerusalem, the apostles, Peter and John, healed a cripple Acts 3:1-10). The apostles performed many signs and wonders among the people, and all those who were sick were healed (Acts 5:12-16). Peter brought Tabitha back from the dead (Acts 9:36-42). A man crippled from birth was healed by the Apostle Paul (Acts 14:10). Eutychus, who fell from a third-storey window, was raised from the dead through the prayers of the apostle Paul (Acts 20:7-12). Publius, the chief official on the island of Malta, was healed through Paul's prayers as were a great many others (Acts 28:7-9).

In the latter days that we are living, we are experiencing the renewing of the Holy Spirit upon the church as prophesied by the prophet Joel (Joel 2:28-32). Many believe we are witnessing the latter rains and anointing of the Holy Spirit.[126] Indeed, today there are many testimonies of healing and miracles occurring in churches across the world.[127, 128, 129] Jesus is coming soon, even now, come Lord Jesus (Revelation 22:20).

---

126. Derek Prince. *Prophetic Guide to the End Times: Facing the Future Without Fear.* Chapter 13: "The objectives of the end time church," pp. 181-182. Chosen Books, Grand Rapids, MI, USA, 2008.
127. "The complete school of healing and miracles."
https://healingandmiracles.com/testimonies-of-healing/
128. Jack Hayford. https://www.jackhayford.org/teaching/articles/my-personal-testimony-of-healing/
129. Andrew Wommack. *Discover the Keys to Staying Full of God.* Chapter 4: "What do you value?," pp. 25-35. Andrew Wommack Ministries Europe, Walsall, UK, 2008.

Prayer

Dear Heavenly Father, we thank you that you are a God that heals our ailments, diseases and anxieties. We are grateful that you love us and care for us. Although you are Almighty God, from everlasting to everlasting, the creator of the universe, you show compassion upon us, not wanting any to be lost but for all to be saved and to be in heaven with you. Dear Lord, we are thankful that you came to earth to reconcile us to our God, and to show us the way to eternal life. We are thankful, Father, that even though we shall die, we will be raised to eternal life and are destined to be in paradise with you. We thank you, Father, that nothing is impossible for you. Thank you, Jesus, that while we are on the earth, we are able to accomplish even greater things than you through the ministry of the Holy Spirit. We claim our healing from everything that bothers us and makes us afraid whether it be incurable human diseases like cancer, or mental health issues. We are thankful to know that nothing is too difficult for you and for those who have faith in you. In Jesus's name we pray, Amen.

11.

The power of God

THE POWER OF GOD can be shown through the fact that nothing is impossible for God (Matthew 19:26). I will provide a few examples of the power of God and of God achieving the impossible here.

God the creator

In the beginning, Jesus was with God and was God, and through him, all things were made (John 1:1-2). This account by itself tells us the power of God that he made all things; nothing existed before God created it. The earth was formless and full of darkness before God spoke and then we have light (Genesis 1:1-3). God created the universe by merely speaking the word and it was done (Genesis 1:14-19; Psalm 33:6). What is mankind compared with the vastness and the greatness of the universe that

God cares for and loves us (Psalm 8:3-4)? God created and named the stars and God will create a new heaven and a new earth at the end of this age (Psalm 147:4; Isaiah 65:17). All things hold together through God (Colossians 1:16-17). Not a single star or solar system is missing because God holds them in place (Isaiah 40:26).

Since the creation of the world, God's invisible qualities are clear for everyone to see, and there will be no excuses on judgement day when all men and women stand before the throne of God to say that we did not know of God's existence (Romans 1:20). The workings of the universe are hidden from the wise but revealed to little children (Matthew 11:25). This is certainly true when mathematicians, physicists, philosophers and other academics struggle to explain the workings of the universe, when in fact, the simple answer is that God created the heavens and the earth.[130] However, the Bible tells us that it is only through faith that we can accept that the universe was formed at God's command (Hebrews 11:3).

The flood

The wickedness and evil in human hearts grieved God and God planned to wipe mankind from the earth (Genesis 6:5-7). The survival of mankind was brought about

---

130. For an overview on the current thinking regarding the creation of the universe, see Stephen Hawking. *A Brief History of Time*, updated edition. Penguin Books, London, UK, 2016. For an overview of the arguments surrounding creation and evolution, see Aaron R. Yilmaz. *Deliver Us from Evolution*. Amazon Books, 2019.

through one man; the righteousness of Noah (Genesis 6:9). The Bible tells us that everything on dry land was drowned during the flood apart from those who found refuge with Noah in the ark (Genesis 7:23).

It is perhaps surprising that geologists and historians have found evidence of a widespread flood in Mesopotamia, China, India, the Mayan Kingdom and Peru among other nations.[131] After the flood had lasted 150 days, God remembered Noah and his family and the flood receded (Genesis 8:1).

Mankind was then free to go out and multiply and occupy the earth. It is of interest in these days of scepticism regarding the accuracy of the Biblical account, that creation stories of many countries across the earth begin with chaotic waters receding across the land.[132] Yuval Noah Harari believes that mankind was responsible for the mass extinctions of many animal species, such as mammoths and other large animals and marsupials,[133] as mankind learned to master the sea by building boats, and learned to expand across the earth. Perhaps this fact fits in with scientists estimating that 99% of animals that ever lived on the planet are now extinct.[134] Harari calls mankind's expansion across the earth "one of the biggest and swiftest ecological

---

131. Susan Wise Bauer. *The History of the Ancient World.* Chapter 2: "The earliest story," pp. 10-16. Norton Press, New York, USA, 2007.

132. Ibid.

133. Yuval Noah Harari. *Sapiens: A Brief History of Humankind.* Chapter 4: "The flood," pp. 70-83. Vintage, Penguin Random House, London, UK, 2011.

134. "Uncommon Descent, have 99% of all species gone extinct?" June 2009. https://uncommondescent.com/evolution/have-99-of-all-species-gone-extinct/

disasters to befall the animal kingdom." Harari concludes his chapter on the flood by telling us that among large animals, the only survivors of mankind's expansion across the earth will be humans themselves and the farmyard animals that served as slaves in Noah's ark.

The main point of the flood is that God was grieved by the wickedness of mankind, and God has the power to destroy the evil he sees emerging across the world. The goodness of God can be seen in the covenant that God made with Noah never to send another worldwide flood to destroy mankind and the land-based animals that require air to breathe (Genesis 9:11-17). It is worth reminding ourselves that God created a rainbow to remind himself not to send another flood.

Miraculous birth

When we think of miraculous birth, we immediately think of the immaculate birth of Jesus in the manger in Bethlehem. However, before this birth was the birth of Isaac (Genesis 21:1-7). The promise that was made to Abraham and Sarah was that even though they were well past child-bearing age, they would have a son. The miracle not only shows the faithfulness of God to keep his promise, but it reinforces the fact that nothing is impossible with God, and that God is not bound by the laws of science. God promised to bring into being a nation from Isaac which were to be his chosen people Israel. The creation of Israel indicates the extent of God's planning that before the foundation of the earth, God planned for his chosen people. It is never a game of chance with God. Israel is God's chosen possession, not because they are more numerous than other nations, but because God simply loved them, and God honoured the promise he made to Abraham (Deuteronomy 7:6-8).

Yet, there are three other births that are important in the history of Israel, and these are the birth of Moses, who led Israel out of slavery, Obed, who was the father of Jesse, who was the father of David, and thirdly, the birth of Samuel, who led Israel in a new direction. All three births show that God does not leave anything to chance.

The power of God is shown most clearly in the conceiving of Jesus through the Holy Spirit (Luke 1:26-38; Luke 2:1-7). Above all, it shows that God is above and beyond the laws of science, and the best explanation for the birth of Jesus is the Biblical account.

God's power over the earth

There are many different accounts within the Bible which would illustrate God's power over the earth, but the one that I would focus upon is the account in Joshua, Chapter 10. The story is based upon the people of Gibeon making a peace agreement with Israel. This peace agreement angered the Kings of Jerusalem, Hebron, Jarmuth, Lachish and Eglon, all Amorite Kings, so they joined forces and attacked Gibeon. The Gibeonites appealed for help from the Israelites and Joshua came to their rescue.

The Israelites routed the Amorites, and God chipped in by sending huge hailstones on the retreating Amorites which killed more Amorites than the soldiers of Israel. However, to ensure the victory was complete and was not curtailed by night time setting which would have allowed the Amorites to escape, Joshua asked God to stop the sun (Joshua 10:12-13). God obliged and the sun did not move for a whole day, and Joshua completed the destruction of the Amorites.

What fascinates me about this account is that three researchers from Ben Gurion University believe they have discovered the scientific explanation behind the miraculous Biblical account of the sun standing still for Joshua during the battle, which they attribute to a solar eclipse. Using data from NASA, the researchers were able to pinpoint the battle to October 12, 1207 BCE.[135] What is interesting here is that more and more accounts from the Bible, particularly the Old Testament, which until recently were dismissed as myths or fables, are now being proven to be accurate historical accounts. The other consideration here is that God sent a solar eclipse and stopped night from forming at the exact moment Joshua needed and requested God's help.

---

135. "Scientists discover exact date of Joshua's Biblical battle against five kings." *Israel365 News.* https://www.israel365news.com/82306/scientists-discover-joshua-stopped-sun/

Power of God—don't doubt the floodgates

Ben-Hadad, the king of Aram, was at war with Israel and besieged Samaria causing a great famine (2 Kings 6:24-33). The king of Israel blamed the prophet Elisha for the predicament that Israel found itself in and threatened to behead Elisha. However, Elisha promised that the siege would be lifted and there would be an abundance of food within the next 24 hours. One of the soldiers disbelieved the prophet and doubted that even if God opened the floodgates of heaven that there would be such an abundance of food (2 Kings 7:2). Needless to say, God opened the floodgates and there was an abundance of food as the prophet predicted, but the soldier who doubted was crushed to death as the starving people rushed to get the food (2 Kings 7:17-19). The moral of the story is that when we receive a message from God, believe in his power to deliver the answer. Too often, we look to the circumstances of our situation rather than relying on the power of God to deliver us from the famines of life.

God also brought deliverance to Jerusalem when the Assyrian King Sennacherib besieged the city (2 Kings 18:17-37). When the Assyrians sent a letter to the Israelite King Hezekiah, the king read the letter and then went to the Temple to bring the letter before God (2 Kings 19:14-19). How often when we receive bad news do we take it before God? Often, we don't look to God at all but panic and get depressed. The reason for not turning to God is usually our lack of belief in his ability to deliver us from evil. We are too often dependent on our own resources and fail to engage the power of God in our daily lives. Isaiah, the prophet, promised King Hezekiah that Jerusalem would be delivered from the Assyrians and that very night, God sent his angel to put to death 185,000 Assyrian soldiers thus lifting the siege (2 Kings 19:35-36).

God's power through the miracles of Jesus

C. S. Lewis defines miracles as an interference with nature (scientific laws) by a supernatural power,[136] namely God or his son, our Lord and Saviour Jesus Christ. Charles Ryrie states that four words are used in the gospels to describe Jesus's miracles: Dunamis, illustrating the almighty power of God; Teras, describing a sign or wonder performed by Christ; Ergon, describing the works and mercy of Jesus; and Semeion, a sign to teach a spiritual truth.[137] Ryrie describes 35 miracles that Jesus performed during his life on earth and emphasises that each miracle was performed to meet the specific needs of others.[138] I am not going to go through all the miracles Jesus performed but will illustrate God's power through the miracles described in John's gospel.

John selected seven signs in his gospel as illustrations of the power of Jesus over the world. John did assert that

---

136. C. S. Lewis. *Miracles*. Chapter 2: "The naturalist and the supernatural-ist," p. 5. Collins Publishers, London, UK, 2012 edition.
137. Charles C. Ryrie. *The Miracles of our Lord*. "Introduction," p. 10. Loizeaux Brothers edition, USA, 1988.
138. Ibid., pp. 10-11.

he was aware of a far greater number of miracles that Jesus performed during his earthly mission.[139] The seven signs that John chose were as follows: water being changed into wine at a wedding in Cana (John 2:1-11) which illustrates the quality Jesus is able to bring to our lives: the healing of the nobleman's son (John 4:46-54) which illustrates the power that God has over distance. The nobleman believed Jesus healed his son even though he had travelled a long distance to find Jesus and despite how far away the son was: the healing of a man by the pool (John 5:1-18) showing Jesus's authority over time: the feeding of the five thousand (John 6:1-14) demonstrating Jesus's power over quantity: Jesus walking on water (John 6:16-21) emphasising Jesus's authority over nature and science: the healing of the blind man (John 9:1-41) describing Jesus's authority over misfortune: the raising of Lazarus (John 11:1-44) exemplifying Jesus's power over death.[140]

The two greatest miracles in the New Testament are undoubtedly the resurrection of Jesus, providing a new life for all who believe in Jesus as their Lord and Saviour, and the ascension of Jesus into heaven to sit at the right hand of God. In this respect, the best is yet to come as we look to Jesus's return to the earth to claim his own.

---

139. Merrill C. Tenney. *John: The Gospel of Belief: An Analytic Study of the Text*, pp. 311-313. Eerdmans, Grand Rapids, MI, USA, 1997.
140. For a fuller explanation of the miracles in John's gospel, see Merrill C. Tenney, ibid.

The power of God as illustrated in the day of the Lord

At the end, there will be a time of distress such as never seen before since the first nations were formed (Daniel 12:1). Everyone whose name is written in God's Book of Life will be delivered from the apocalypse (Daniel 12:1-2).

What is occurring on the earth now and what will occur in the days of distress? We are warned not to be deceived because many will come in the name of Jesus as false prophets and false messiahs; there will be wars and rumours of wars; nation will rise against nation and ethnic groups against each other; we can expect an increase in famines and earthquakes and other natural disasters as the earth is overwhelmed with global warming and the like; Christians will be handed over to death and will be betrayed by fellow Christians presumably so that they can escape execution themselves; there will be an increase in evil and many false prophets will arise; the gospel will be preached to every nation before the end comes (Matthew 24:4-14).

To illustrate the power of God, we should look at the seven seals and the seven trumpets that are described in the book of Revelation. Jesus in heaven will open the seven seals which will release A conquest of nations; peace will be removed from the earth and armies will kill each other; the price of wheat and barley will increase due to the shortage and I wonder with the current war between Ukraine and Russia whether we will see this occurring in the coming days, especially as so much of the world's wheat and grain is produced by Russia and Ukraine; a quarter of the earth will die due to famine, plagues, gun crime and killed by wild beasts; the sun will turn black and there will be a great earthquake, and the stars will fall to earth (Revelation 6:1-15). When I first became a Christian in 1974, I could not imagine seeing any of these events in my lifetime, but now in 2022, these events appear very close. Perhaps the saddest thing is that at the end, so many people will hide in caves, and call on the mountains and rocks to fall upon them to hide themselves from the face of the living God (Revelation 7:15-17).

Seven angels with seven trumpets

There is worse to come at the sound of heavenly trumpets (Revelation 8, 9 and 11). At the first trumpet, there came hail and fire and blood and a third of the earth was destroyed by fire. Again, we see large forest fires in many areas of the world. In California, USA, in 2021, there were 8,835 fires which burnt over 2.5 million acres of land and wildfires are increasing in California due to global warming.[141] In May 2022, President Biden declared the fires in New Mexico a disaster.[142] Wildfires raging in Argentina in 2022 are responsible for destroying homes and chasing animals out of their natural habitat.[143] The combination of extremely high temperatures (>45ºC) resulted

---

141. https://en.wikipedia.org/wiki/2021_California_wildfires
142. https://www.greenmatters.com/p/wildfires-new-mexico
143. https://www.greenmatters.com/p/argentina-wildfires

in 2.5 times the annual number of wildfires (1,877 as of August 10, 2021) in Southern Europe.[144] Wildfires in Australia resulted in dozens of people dying in Australia's 2019-2020 bushfire season, which was one of the worst on record. More than 10 million hectares of land burned and over a billion animals are estimated to have died, with many species pushed close to extinction.[145] It is surprising that the Bible was able to predict these events more than 2,000 years ago.

The second trumpet sounded and mountains were thrown into the sea and a third of the sea creatures died, probably due to the toxicity caused by the mountains falling into the sea.

Given that many volcanoes are named as mountains, such as Mount Vesuvius and Mount Etna, it is not difficult to imagine a scenario where erupting volcanoes fall into the sea and cause devastation. Mount Etna is an active volcano in southern Europe; however, eruptions aren't the only major threat posed by this volcano. A new study shows that Etna is slowly sliding toward the sea, raising the prospect that it may suddenly collapse and cause a huge tsunami that could devastate the region around the eastern Mediterranean Sea.[146]

---

144. https://www.weforum.org/agenda/2021/08/extreme-fire-season-in-europe/
145. https://edition.cnn.com/2021/03/18/australia/australia-wildfires-smoke-volcano-intl-hnk-scn/index.html
146. "Mount Etna is sliding into the sea. History shows that could be catastrophic." https://www.nbcnews.com/mach/science/mount-etna-sliding-sea-history-shows-could-be-catastrophic-ncna925051

The Cumbre Vieja volcano on the island of La Palma in the Canary Islands erupted in September 2021 and authorities were concerned about what might happen if lava from the volcano reached the Atlantic Ocean.[147] Experts were concerned that the lava mixing with the salt water of the ocean might cause explosions from thermal shock as the lava has a temperature of around 1,800ºF (1,100ºC) and the seawater just 73ºF (23ºC). The mixture of the molten rock and the seawater might trigger toxic reactions, but there were also concerns that the reaction could destabilise the coastline causing it to collapse into the ocean. There were similar concerns regarding the eruption of the Kilauea volcano in Hawaii in 2019 because if lava meets the saltwater of the ocean, it can create "laze" which is full of hydrochloric acid and fine lava particles.[148] There are many other active volcanoes around the world and there are concerns that eruptions from volcanoes, especially those so-called super volcanoes, could trigger catastrophic effects across the planet.

When the third trumpet sounded, a large star called bitterness fell out of the sky into a third of the rivers across the world contaminating the drinking water and anyone who drank from the contaminated water died (Revelation 8:10-11). This kind of toxicity could quite easily be caused by a nuclear war like the one Russia is threatening

---

147. "La Palma volcano: What will happen when the lava reaches the Atlantic Ocean." https://en.as.com/en/2021/09/23/latest news/1632351745_463920.html

148. Concerns regarding the Kilauea volcano in Hawaii. https://www.inverse.com/article/46466-kilauea-volcano-ocean-entry-deemed-hazardous-as-dangerous-laze-persists

as I write. Should a limited nuclear attack take place, it is not inconceivable that radioactive material could get into the water table and contaminate drinking water. The sounding of the fourth trumpet resulted in a third of the sun losing its light; a third of the moon and stars were also darkened (Revelation 8:12). At the sounding of the fifth trumpet, a star fell to earth and opened the abyss releasing locusts that are given permission to attack all people who do not have the seal of God (Revelation 9:1-6). The stings from the locusts were so excruciating that they caused men to want to die. The seal of God is the Holy Spirit living inside of all who believe and have accepted Jesus as our Lord and Saviour (Ephesians 1:13-14).

At the sounding of the fifth trumpet, it released four angels who had been held back at the river Euphrates (Revelation 9:13-21). An army of 200 million was released and a third of mankind was murdered during the conflict. Sadly, the 75% of mankind that were not killed in this conflict did not repent of their idolatry or worshipping demons; they were also thieves, sexually immoral, and into the occult. At the sounding of the seventh trumpet, the Kingdom of Jesus comes and his reign will be forever and ever (Revelation 11:15-19).

Seven plagues and seven bowls of God's wrath

It is not my intention to go through the whole of Revelation in detail, but just those parts which highlight the power of God in the last days of the earth.

It is pertinent to be ready for the last days and there will be no excuse for those who have rejected God's gift of salvation through our Lord Jesus Christ. It is also important to emphasize here that those who are sealed with the Holy Spirit and still on the earth will not be harmed by the wrath of God. Revelation 7 describes the 144,000 who were sealed from the 12 tribes of Israel. Revelation 7 also describes the great multitude of Christians who have been raptured and standing before the throne of God before the wrath of God comes upon the earth. Jesus stated that when the gospel has been preached to every nation, the end will come (Matthew 24:14), and we are told that the multitude before God's throne in heaven are from every nation (Revelation 7:9-11). The great multitude have been raptured and are in heaven before the seven trumpets are sounded, and before the seven plagues and bowls of God's wrath are poured out upon the earth.

We are not told what the seven plagues are but we have already witnessed the emergence of plagues on the earth in recent times, such as Covid-19, SARS, Ebola and Monkeypox, and there is a constant fear of avian influenza crossing the species barrier infecting man and causing a pandemic that is even greater than the 1918-1919 influenza pandemic that was estimated to have killed 50 million people.[149]

---

149. Andrew Nikiforuk. *The Fourth Horseman: A Short History of Epidemics, Plagues and Other Scourges.* Chapter 8: "Influenza viral waves," p. 146. Phoenix Orion Books Ltd., London, UK, 1992. Mark Honigsbaum. *The Pandemic Century: A History of Global Contagion from the Spanish Flu to Covid-19.* Chapter 1: "The blue death" p. 8. Penguin Random House, London, UK, 2020.

The seven bowls of God's wrath can be summarised as follows (Revelation 16): The seven angels each pour out their bowls in the following order:

1. On the land and a painful skin infection broke out on all those who had the mark of the beast.
2. Into the sea which became blood and all sea creatures and fauna died.
3. Into the rivers and springs and they turned to blood, because of the shed blood of his people.
4. On the sun and the sun scorched the earth including people who were burnt. Despite this, the people did not repent, which indicates that even at this late stage, there was room for God's mercy.
5. On the throne of the antichrist, and the earth and his domain were plunged into darkness. Those left on the earth were in agony but still refused to repent.
6. On the river Euphrates and the river dried up. This allowed the kings from the East to advance, but it also resulted in the release of evil spirits and demons on the earth from the beast, the dragon and the false prophet. The kings advanced to Armageddon for the final battle.
7. Into the air and God declared from heaven that it was finished. There were multiple natural disasters and the greatest earthquake ever seen which destroyed all the islands and mountains in the world. There was also an enormous hail storm with each hailstone measuring 100 pounds in weight.

We can see the awesome power of Almighty God and it is important to remember that it is a fearful thing to fall into the hands of the living God (Hebrews 10:31). It is also reassuring that for those who are his children through the precious blood of Christ, t we can call him Father. Our Father who is in heaven, blessed be your name, your kingdom is coming upon the earth, and your will be done both in heaven and on the earth (Matthew 6:9-10).

Prayer

Dear Heavenly Father, we acknowledge your awesome power and we are delighted to know that you are in control of everything that is happening upon the earth and that will happen throughout the world as we move towards the end of this age. Thank you that you have revealed to us what is to come so that we need not be afraid of the future. We recognise that there will be wars and rumours of wars, and there will be an increase in famines, earthquakes and other natural disasters as we move toward the end. We look forward to being with you in heaven, Father, as part of your family and sharing eternity with you. Thank you, Jesus, for all that you have done for us, so that through repentance of our old life and accepting you as our Lord and Saviour, we are saved from the wrath to come. In Jesus's name we pray, Amen.

12.

Eternal life

WHEN WE THINK OF paradise, it cannot be compared with earthly pictures. For example, advertisers want us to believe that using a certain shampoo will be paradise or eating a certain type of chocolate bar or buying the car we always wanted. Other illusions of paradise include finding the perfect life partner, the perfect home, or the perfect career move. When Jesus spoke to the thief on the cross of being in paradise today with him (Luke 23:43), he was not comparing paradise with any earthly desire or accomplishment. Jesus was talking about being in heaven and seeing the new heaven and the new earth that God was going to create to accommodate all those who believe in Christ. Jesus promised paradise at a time when both he and the thief were dying the most excruciating death on a cross. Death will eventually come to us all, and, before we die, we need to assess where we would like to spend eternity because the Bible only offers two choices—heaven or hell.

As Roger Ellsworth states in his book on heaven, death comes upon us swiftly and, therefore, we should not delay our decision because we may simply run out of time.[150]

Resurrection

As believers in Christ as our Lord and Saviour, we are waiting for Jesus to come back and claim his bride the church (Revelation 19:7; 21:2). We, as believers in Christ, will be resurrected to be with him, and, in this respect, the Bible describes the resurrection of mankind in several categories as follows:

1. Believers at the time of the rapture. When Christ returns in the clouds. Those who have fallen asleep (the dead) in Christ will be resurrected first because they have waited the longest to be with their Lord and Saviour. Then those who are still alive will be caught up in the clouds to be with the Lord for eternity (1 Thessalonians 4:14-17).
2. Walvoord believes that Israel and the Old Testament saints, at the time of Jesus coming to earth to establish his kingdom, will be a separate group who are resurrected (Daniel 12:2; Hosea 13:13; Matthew 22:30-32).[151]

---

150. Roger Ellsworth. *What the Bible Teaches About Heaven*, pp. 23-28. Evangelical Press, Darlington, UK, 2007. I recommend this book as a good overview of the Biblical views concerning heaven.
151. John F. Walvoord. *Jesus Christ our Lord. The future work of Christ is also dependent on his resurrection*, pp. 215-216. Moody Bible Institute, Chicago, USA, 1969.

3. Walvoord also has those saints who have come to faith through tribulation as a separate group that will be resurrected at the end of time (Revelation 20:4). He would also place the millennial saints in a separate category for resurrection but acknowledges that this group is not selectively mentioned in the Bible for resurrection.

4. The final group to be resurrected are the wicked and those who have chosen darkness over Christ who will be resurrected for judgement at the end of time/millennial reign of Christ (Revelation 20:12-14).[152]

We know that when we meet him, we will be like him and be perfected with a new heavenly body (1 John 3:2). In this respect, the Bible describes mankind as being made up of a body, souls and spirit (1 Thessalonians 5:23). Now, there are views that only our spirits will be resurrected and this cannot be argued from the Bible. In fact, it is a heresy more closely aligned with Gnosticism which was so vehemently opposed by the New Testament authors, particularly Paul in Galatians and Romans and Peter in his epistles. Gnosticism basically taught that the body of mankind is evil and the spirit is good, so anything we do in the body is evil, so effectively, anything goes as the body will be destroyed at death and only the spirit lives on beyond the grave. However, Paul prays that God will sanctify our body, soul and spirit so that we will be faultless at the coming of Jesus (1 Thessalonians 5:23-24).

---

152. Ibid.

Heaven and earth

Once we reach heaven, all our suffering, trials and tribulations will be behind us and we will be delivered from past iniquities and painful memories (Isaiah 65:17). Thankfully, there will be a new heaven, a new earth, and a new Jerusalem (Isaiah 66:22 and Revelation 21:1-11), which is most welcome when we consider how mankind has effectively brought such great destruction on the present earth.

The Bible describes in some detail the paradise which will be found in the new Jerusalem (Revelation 21:15-21). The glory of God will shine down upon the city and there will be no need for a temple or a church building to go and worship because God himself will be inside the heart of every believer. The glory of God will light up the whole universe, and we will all experience the immenseness of God's glory that the universe will shine brighter than any star due to the glory of God. The beauty is that God is light and where God is there can be no darkness (1 John 1:5), therefore, the new heaven and the new earth will never grow dark because God's light reigns forever (Revelation 21:22-24). The new heaven and earth will have a fabric and organisation as the God-appointed kings and rulers will serve God and bring glory to the new heaven and earth. We will be part of a Kingdom that will never diminish (Psalm 145:13).

Paradise in heaven

There will be no more suffering or striving to make ends meet because we shall be in paradise. Every tear will be wiped away, and there will be no more grief or mourning or pain (Revelation 21:4). We will never again go hungry or thirsty, or be burnt by having to toil under the midday sun (Revelation 7:16-17). There will be no more death or humiliation (Isaiah 25:8).

God will sit on the throne of heaven and the purity and holiness of God will be seen by everyone who is in heaven. His throne is surrounded by four living creatures and the 24 elders who continually worship the Lord (Revelation 4:4-11). There will be a great multitude of Christians who have been saved and resurrected through their belief in Jesus as their Lord and Saviour (Revelation 7:1-17). The ark of the covenant will be seen in heaven (Revelation 11:19). There has been a lot of speculation about what happened to the ark of the covenant, whether the Roman Catholic church has the ark in the church archives in Rome, or whether the ark was carried to Ethiopia or some other earthly place. The Bible tells us that God has the ark of the covenant and it is with him in heaven. There will be much rejoicing and worshipping of God for all that he has done in redeeming mankind and bringing believers to eternal life in him (Revelation 19:1-8).

Jesus tells us that the Kingdom of Heaven is like a wedding banquet and that many were invited to the banquet, but a number of those invited refused to come or were too busy with their earthly business to come to the feast (Matthew 22:1-13). However, they enter the heavenly party and to be a part of the banquet everyone has to have a robe of righteousness, and all those without the robe will be bound up and thrown outside into the darkness (Matthew 22:13). For those who are called and enter the Kingdom of God, our filthy rags will be taken away and we will be clothed in clean garments that shine as white as snow (Zechariah 3:3-4, Isaiah 1:18). We will delight in the Lord because we wear the robes of righteousness (Isaiah 61:10). For those who overcome the trials and tribulations of life and call upon the name of the Lord will be given the garment of salvation, and our names are written in God's Book of Life (Revelation 3:5).

Our Father's house

Troubles and worry are a common feature of life in this fallen world that we live in, and on the night before his death, Jesus told the disciple about his Father's mansion (John 14:1-3).[153] We don't have to be weighed down by the trials of this world, because we can look forward to the day when we will have a room in the mansion of God. The message is that this world is not our home or final resting place; paradise awaits. The good news is that Jesus has promised to come and take us to the room prepared for us in our Father's mansion. It is up to us to make

---

153. Roger Ellsworth. *What the Bible Teaches About Heaven*, pp. 79-85. Evangelical Press, Darlington, UK, 2007.

sure that we have treasure in heaven because we will all want to have something wonderful to put in our rooms (Matthew 6:20).[154] Giving to and regarding the poor, the fatherless and the widows among us are important considerations when we consider what heavenly treasure is. The rich young ruler was instructed to give up his possessions and help the poor as a way of entering into the kingdom of God (Matthew 19:21). We are requested to do what is correct by caring for the poor, the widows and orphans (Isaiah 1:17). We are considered faultless and pure if we have regard for widows and orphans and by not being polluted by what the world has to offer (James 1:27). Are we helping the hungry, the thirsty, those who cannot afford clothes, helping strangers and visiting those who need help? For these are the things that separate the righteous from the unrighteous (Matthew 25:31-46).

The new Jerusalem

The new Jerusalem will shine with the glory of God, and its appearance will be crystal clear, and it will be huge by comparison with any city we currently see upon the earth, some 1,400 miles long and the same distance wide (Revelation 21:10-27). The city will be covered in gold and precious stones and there will be no night time so the gates will always be open for us to come and go as God wills. The river of life will flow through the middle of the great city, and the tree of life bearing fruit will be found

---

154. Ibid., p. 107-114.

on either side of the river (Revelation 22:1-5). Most of all, God's and Jesus's thrones will be in the city (Revelation 22:3). There are no words to describe the glorious sight of God's throne, although men have tried (Ezekiel 1:26-28; Daniel 7:9-14; Revelation 4:2-11). It will be a wonderful sight to experience the glory of God and to participate in the worship services that are in heaven. Hallelujah, even come Lord Jesus.

Prayer

Dear heavenly Father, thank you so much that we are part of your family. Praise you that one day we will be in heaven with you and that all our trials and tribulations will be behind us. Thank you that there will be a day when we will be able to participate in the worship services in heaven and to enjoy our room in your mansion. Thank you, Father, that you will wipe away every tear and replace our tears with rejoicing and blessings beyond what we could ever hope or imagine. Thank you, Lord Jesus, that you are coming soon for your children to take us to our heavenly homes. Above all, thank you, Father, that we will be able to experience the new Jerusalem, to see the golden streets, to walk next to the river of life and to eat the fruit from the tree of life. Thank you so much, in Jesus's name we pray, Amen.

Other books available

The book explores seven key areas to the victorious Christian life and remaining free in Christ regardless of the circumstances we find ourselves facing in the coming days. As Christians, we are either afraid of or want to skip over quickly the challenging teachings in the word of God, such as the struggles with and consequences of sin, and the coming wrath of God in order to reach the more positive teachings on salvation and eternal life for all who believe in Jesus as Lord and Saviour.

All of us want to be free from the things that hold us captive in life. Jesus offered us the opportunity to know the truth, and that his truth would set us free. Totally free means being set free to be the person God created us to be, to be free from fear, from circumstances, from the strongholds that tell us that we can never achieve all that we want to achieve. The Bible is the only source of the truth that promises to set us free. This book explores the principles and defines the tenets that allow us to be set free from the strongholds that bind us and try to limit us to less than we are capable of achieving in this life. The book outlines some of the major obstacles that bind us and stop us from being free. The book also indicates how we can find the freedom that Jesus promised through the truth of the Gospel. The book explores twelve areas of the truth of the Christian life and outlines some of the principles needed to remain free in Christ, regardless of the circumstances we find ourselves facing.

John Clarke is an Evangelical Christian based in Wokingham, Berkshire, England. In over 50 years as a Christian,
he has been a member of Baptist, Episcopalian, Evangelical Free, Methodist and Pentecostal fellowships throughout the years. He has lived in Liverpool, Southampton,
Guildford, Reading, Macclesfield and Wokingham in
England and Milan in Italy.